Physical C...
of the Si...

(from the American K...

Shoulders: The shoulder blade is well laid back. The upper arm angles slightly backward from point of shoulder to elbow.

Back: Straight and strong, with a level topline from withers to croup. It is of medium length. The loin is taut and lean, narrower than the rib cage, and with a slight tuck-up. The croup slopes away from the spine at an angle.

Hindquarters: The upper thighs are well muscled and powerful, the stifles well bent, the hock joint well-defined and set low to the ground.

Tail: The well furred tail of fox-brush shape is set on just below the level of the topline.

Color: All colors from black to pure white are allowed. A variety of markings on the head is common, including many striking patterns not found in other breeds.

Height: Dogs, 21 to 23.5 inches at the withers. Bitches, 20 to 22 inches at the withers.

Weight: Dogs, 45 to 60 pounds. Bitches, 35 to 50 pounds.

Coat: Double and medium in length, giving a well furred appearance. The undercoat is soft and dense and of sufficient length to support the outer coat.

Siberian Husky

◇

by Lorna Winslette

Contents

KENNEL CLUB BOOKS® SIBERIAN HUSKY
ISBN: 1-59378-209-8

Copyright © 2003, 2007 • Kennel Club Books® A Division of BowTie, Inc.
40 Broad Street, Freehold, New Jersey 07728 USA
Cover Design Patented: US 6,435,559 B2 • Printed in South Korea

Photo Credits:
Norvia Behling, Carolina Biological Supply, Kent and Donna Dannen, Doskocil, Isabelle Français, James Hayden-Yoav, James R Hayden, RBP, Carol Ann Johnson, Dwight R. Kuhn, Dr. Dennis Kunkel, Mikki Pet Products, Phototake, Jean Claude Revy, Nikki Sussman, Alice van Kempen and C. James Webb.

Illustrations by Reneé Low.

10 9 8 7 6 5 4

HISTORY OF THE
SIBERIAN HUSKY

GENESIS AND ORIGINAL PURPOSE OF THE BREED

Several thousand years ago, primitive Eskimo-like tribes in Siberia used dogs for specific functions in everyday life. These dogs were essential to the humans' survival as they performed vital tasks, which included accompanying the hunters, scenting trails and helping to transport food back to the villages. Each tribe had its own specific type, which at this point was a precursor to a specific breed of dog, but all of the Northern dogs were similar in the sense of being jackal-type dogs that, at one time, had been crossbred with Arctic wolves. Of course, this was thousands of years ago, and through careful breeding and maintenance of pure bloodlines, the "wolf" was bred out of the dog. The pure-bred Siberian Husky of today is not a wild wolf hybrid, as anyone close to the breed will attest, but a beautiful, friendly, tractable, wonderful dog in both pet and working capacities.

In Siberia, the ancestors of the Husky were originally used for hunting until another use for them evolved. Each tribe bred and maintained its own specific type of dog. These Northern dogs eventually evolved into the distinct breeds that we know today: the Alaskan Malamute, Eskimo Dog and Samoyed, to name a few. The Chukchi tribe is credited with the origination of the dog that we have come to

NORTHERN BREEDS

The Northern breeds of dog, typified by the Siberian Husky, share many physical characteristics, including the prick, well-furred ears; brush curled tails; thick double coats and pointy

THE AKITA

muzzles. Among the celebrated Northern breeds we have the Alaskan Malamute, Samoyed, Finnish Spitz, Akita and Eskimo Dog. In addition to pulling sleds, Northern dogs earned their daily fish by hunting, herding and guarding the family.

(FACING PAGE)
A few thousand years ago, Siberian inhabitants of the deep snows developed types of dogs as companions, workers, guards and transporters of food.

was born! In addition to accompanying the tribesmen to the sea and bringing home food, the sled dogs were used for transporting goods and trading between tribes, and for hauling the tribe's possessions if they had to relocate to a more hospitable region.

The Husky, then referred to as the Siberian Chukchi, or simply the Chukchi, was bred mainly for endurance rather than for speed or strength. The dogs were bred specifically to pull light loads at medium speeds; heavier loads required teams of dogs. The most important thing was that they were able to withstand the long distances and transport their cargo intact. The dogs had to be very energy-efficient in that they had to perform their task with as little effort as possible; they needed to have energy left over to keep their bodies warm in the

know as the Siberian Husky. The Chukchis inhabited the part of Siberia closest to Alaska; at one time the climate was not so harsh, but weather conditions changed for the worse, forcing the tribe to venture further from their settlement to find food. The tribe lived inland, but they came to depend on the sea for food. Thus arose the necessity for a method of transporting the food over the considerable distance, and the sled became that ever-important method of transport. Hence, the "sled dog"

The Greenland Dog, a rare Arctic breed developed on the frigid island of Greenland, might have figured in the ancestry of the Siberian Husky.

below-freezing temperatures.

The Chukchi people were meticulous in their maintenance of the dogs' pure bloodlines. Only the best male lead dogs were bred; the rest of the males were castrated. The dogs had to have almost endless endurance, superb scenting ability, thick woolly coats to protect from the harsh climate, extreme tractability and willingness to obey. The breed today is recognized as one of the friendliest, and is especially known for being good with children. This has much to

The Northern breeds originated as dogs that had been crossbred with Arctic wolves. As specific breeds, including the Siberian Husky, developed and pure bloodlines were maintained, the wolf was eventually bred out of the dogs.

SIBERIAN BREEDS
The Siberian Husky is not the only pure-bred dog that hails from Siberia!

THE WEST SIBERIAN LAIKA

The Fédération Cynologique Internationale (FCI) also registers the West Siberian Laika and the East Siberian Laika. The Western dog is by far the more numerous. These are hard-working hunting and sledding dogs.

do with how the tribespeople treated the dogs. The Chukchi women and children were responsible for the dogs' daily care, so the dogs adapted to family life and became accustomed to much interaction with humans. The children were encouraged to play with the dogs. Today Siberian Huskies are regarded as excellent family pets—very playful and always ready to make a new friend.

INTRODUCTION TO THE UNITED STATES
Although originated in Siberia, the Siberian Husky is generally thought of as an American breed since it was here that these dogs first gained recognition as a separate breed rather than just

another type of Arctic dog. Before their introduction to the States via Alaska, which at that time was not yet a state, Huskies were favored by Russian explorers, who brought the dogs along while charting the Siberian coastline. Still known as Chukchis, the dogs were brought to Alaska in late 1908 by a Russian fur trader named Goosak to be entered in the first All-Alaska Sweepstakes sled dog race. It was a 408-mile race with a first prize of $10,000. The people were unimpressed by Goosak's dogs—they were small in comparison to the sled-dogs they were used to seeing.

Goosak persuaded a driver named Louis Thrustrup to lead his team and, despite tremendous odds against them, the team placed a close third. The first sweepstakes race was just the beginning. Dogsled racing as a sport was becoming very popular, and the Siberian dogs quickly earned a reputation as top-notch sled dogs. Following this race, a Scotsman by the name of Fox Maule Ramsay was so taken with the Chukchi dogs that he chartered a boat to cross the Bering Sea to Siberia and returned with over 60 of the best Arctic dogs he could find. In the third All-Alaska race, two teams of Ramsay's dogs placed first and second. Ramsay himself was the driver of the second-place team.

A very well-known story that documents the Siberian Husky's unparalleled skill as a sled dog is the story of what has come to be known as the "great serum run" of 1925. An outbreak of diphtheria in

---

DRAFTING DOGS

The Arctic Circle has yielded many talented drafting dogs of Northern type. Lappland, not far from central Siberia, produced the Lapphund, an abundantly coated Northern dog

THE FINNISH LAPPHUND

originally used to herd reindeer. Today these dogs, divided into three distinct breeds, the Swedish Lapphund, the Lapinporokoira and the Finnish Lapphund, are companion dogs as well as herders.

Nome, Alaska necessitated the delivery of anti-toxin to prevent further spread of the disease, yet severe weather conditions made it impossible to transport

(FACING PAGE) Often confused with the Siberian Husky is the alluring Alaskan Malamute. Malamutes and Huskies were used for the same purposes.

it by air. The nearest supply of serum, which was in Anchorage, Alaska, could be transported by rail only as far as the town of Nenana, but there were still over 650 miles to travel to reach Nome. The only feasible way to cover the remaining distance, it seemed, was to use teams of sled dogs. The relay teams covered the distance in just five-and-a-half days, which was a remarkably short time to cover such a distance, and the serum was delivered to Nome in time to save the people from what would have resulted in certain death.

IDITAROD TRAIL RACE

Since 1967, Huskies have impressed the world at the Iditarod Trail Race, the world's longest sled-dog race, stretching across Alaska for 1,049 miles. To severely understate this competition, it is an extremely challenging endeavor for man and dog, or woman and dog! Female mushers, beginning with Libby Riddles, have won this great race. More recently, Susan Butcher has won the race several times.

Word of the dogs' incredible endurance and heroism in the face of below-freezing tempera-

Like the closely related Finnish Lapphund, the Swedish Lapphund, shown here, is a Northern dog from Lappland who was originally intended to herd reindeer.

Chinook dogs originated with the Chinook Indians who inhabited the Columbia River area of the northwestern United States. These three Chinook puppies are fine examples of the breed, which is associated with Siberian Husky history.

tures and blizzard-like conditions spread quickly. The names of the dogs and their drivers became household words. Two drivers in particular, Gunner Kaassen and Leonhard Seppala, who used teams of Siberian Huskies, became especially well known. Kaassen's team was the last relay team, the team that delivered the serum to Nome on February 2, 1925. His lead dog, Balto, who had already proven his worth as a sled dog and scenter many times over, became recognized as the finest lead dog in Alaska. In fact, today a statue of Balto stands in New York City's Central Park as a symbol of the serum relay and to commemorate all of the fine dogs that participated. Seppala and his team garnered recognition for covering over 300 miles on the journey to Nome, the longest distance covered by any single team in the relay.

ESTABLISHMENT OF THE BREED

Following the serum relay, Leonard Seppala toured the United States with a group of dogs, most of them Siberian Huskies, to give sled-dog demonstrations. Note that the word "husky" was used as a generic name for all of the sled-dog breeds. The Chukchi dog was first given the name "Siberian Husky" by Americans. These demonstrations gave the Arctic dogs widespread exposure and sparked interest in the Siberian Husky. There was even a sled-dog demonstration

WHAT'S IN A NAME?

The term "husky" is a generic term referring to any Northern-type snow dog. It derives as a bastardization of the word "Eskie" for Eskimo; the Eskimos continue to depend on sled dogs for survival.

at the 1932 Olympic Games in Lake Placid, New York. After completing his exhibition tour, Seppala settled in New England and started racing extensively with his dogs. Not only did he establish himself as a top sled-dog driver but he also helped establish the Siberian Husky in the eastern United States through his own breeding program. Seppala bred his dogs and they became foundation stock for other New England breeders. The Seppala name is known by everyone in Huskies today; in fact, all American-Kennel-Club-registered Siberian Huskies can be traced back to Seppala bloodlines.

New England became home to a concentration of quality Siberian Husky kennels, Arthur Walden's Chinook Kennels in New Hampshire being one of the most important. Walden had already been breeding sled dogs when Seppala arrived with his huskies. Again, these dogs were smaller than those that were being produced in the area and

people immediately discounted their skill as sled dogs. However, as soon as the dogs started racing, people took notice. Seppala's dogs consistently, and handily, beat the local dogs in sled races. Walden, with the help of Milton and Eva "Short" Seeley, produced quality Siberian Huskies based on Alaskan stock, some of which came directly from Leonard Seppala.

Lorna Demidoff established the prominent Monadnock Kennel, also in New Hampshire. Her first champion was a dog she acquired from Chinook, and she followed with many homebred champions and top racing dogs. It is important to note that both Lorna Demidoff and Short Seeley were not only top breeders but top sled-dog drivers as well—they are two of the top women drivers of all time.

The focus of the New England kennels was to preserve the Siberian Husky's working ability while producing dogs that were esthetically pleasing and could win in the conformation ring. The Chukchis' breeding program focused on function rather than form; for example, the dog's beautiful woolly coats were intended to insulate the dogs' bodies, not to be admired by show fanciers. The tribe needed the dogs for survival; they had no need for a beautiful dog. Dog fanciers, however, with intense interest in showing dogs as well as racing them, wanted the best of both worlds—they wanted the best-quality and best-looking dogs possible. Even with an emphasis on beauty, the New England breed is sometimes called by that name in England although the breed's official name worldwide is Siberian Husky.

THE SIBERIAN HUSKY IN GREAT BRITAIN

The Siberian Husky was recognized as a breed in Great

Samoyeds were developed by Mongolian people, who are also called Samoyeds, of northern Russia. The dogs were used mainly for herding.

kennels still managed consistently to produce dogs that were some of the finest racing sled dogs around.

The breed was recognized as the Siberian Husky by the American Kennel Club in 1930; the first AKC-registered Siberian Husky was named Fairbanks Princess Chena. The breed is recognized by America's "other" registry, the United Kennel Club, as the Arctic Husky. Today the

Britain in 1968. The first registered Siberian Husky was Yeso Pack's Tasha, an American bitch who belonged to Lt. Commander William Cracknell. When she was first brought over from the U.S., there was a rabies scare in England that necessitated her being held in quarantine for a lengthy period. Upon her release, the Siberian Husky was designated as a separate breed and she was registered. A

PROTECTIVE TAIL

The Siberian Husky, like all other Northern breeds of dog, boasts a full brush tail that is carried over the dog's back. Although the standard

does not state why this is an important characteristic of the Siberian Husky, evolution explains. This abundantly coated brush tail could easily protect the Husky's face from snow and wind when the dog curls up on the ground. This type of tail, therefore, is a vital component for a dog destined to work and sleep outdoors in Arctic conditions.

normal length of six months, more Siberian Huskies began to be imported into England.

Don and Liz Leich were the first British fanciers to make strides in establishing the breed. They brought back Siberians from the U.S. in 1971 and started a kennel of their own, which produced some dogs who were very successful in the show ring. Like all true breed enthusiasts, they strived to keep their dogs' working ability intact and keen.

The Siberian Husky in England had a slow but steady following, but by 1986 the breed was fully recognized and able to compete for championships. Many breeders have since done very well with the breed and Siberian Huskies are making great strides as pets and show dogs in England.

THE SIBERIAN HUSKY IN SWITZERLAND

The first record of a Siberian Husky in Switzerland was in 1955. In 1963, the Swiss Club for Northern Dogs was founded. This organization discouraged crossbreeding and firmly regulated which dogs were of breeding quality. First of all, in order for a dog to even receive papers, his parents both must have been deemed worthy of breeding. Then the dog must undergo a stringent series of

mate for her was imported from the U.S., and when Cracknell returned to the States with the two Huskies, the puppies from their two matings were left in England. When the quarantine period was restored to the

x-rays, health tests and temperament tests. The club records all
of this information and
determines which dogs and
bitches are approved for use in
breeding programs and which
ones are not allowed to be used
for breeding. The club's
standards are very high and
their regulations strict, but their
policies have ensured consistency in the breed throughout
the years and have assured that
the breed's bloodlines have been
kept pure. The quality of the
Swiss Siberian Huskies is
recognized throughout Europe
and many of these dogs have
been imported into other
European countries to help
improve the quality of the local
Husky stock.

You do not have to
participate in sled
racing to own a
Siberian Husky. The
Husky is such a
beautiful dog,
usually with striking
eyes, that it has
become a favorite
all over the world.

CHARACTERISTICS OF THE
SIBERIAN HUSKY

A FRIEND FOR LIFE

Siberian Huskies are known all over the world as being friendly, playful dogs who make great family pets. Remember that the Chukchi people who originated the breed raised the dogs in a family atmosphere in the midst of their homes and with their children. The dogs grew up knowing that they were part of a family, just as your Siberian Husky will want to be an integral part of your family. The Siberian Husky will be loyal to those in his family, but he will still remain friendly to everyone he meets. In fact, a Siberian Husky can never have too many friends.

This being said, it is no surprise that the Siberian Husky has earned a reputation for being one of the friendliest and most people-oriented breeds around! If you are looking for a guard dog or an ominous presence in your home to ward off strangers, then you better keep looking…the Husky is more likely to greet an intruder with a friendly lick than a menacing bark. The dogs' even temperament and ability to get along with people has to do with their background; the dogs were raised by the women and children of the Chukchi tribe and, therefore, they are used to being around people and being cared for.

Huskies are also very tractable in that they had to be extremely amenable to discipline in order to perform their intended tasks. The sled driver had to have the utmost confidence in his dogs, since he depended on his dogs to be able to reliably scent a trail and find their way to food and back to

(FACING PAGE) A pair of working Siberian Huskies from the Netherlands. These two dogs are at opposite ends of the spectrum in terms of coat color, markings and eye color.

Huskies are noted for their friendliness to people. They were developed to assist their owners, who depended upon the dogs for their very lives.

the village. When man and dog are out on the frozen tundra, there are no signs to tell them which way to turn and no gas stations at which to stop for directions—getting lost in those conditions presents a life-threatening situation. Today, however, the most strenuous "food hunt" that the pet Husky will probably engage in consists of something along the lines of a walk to the corner store with his owner, but trainability and dependability are still very much a part of the breed's character.

Siberian Huskies don't just take well to training—they require it. Huskies *need* discipline. A sled-dog driver had to rely on his dogs' ability to respond to his voice commands. These dogs had to be dependable to a fault, especially the lead dog. Thus, Huskies look to a leader to provide them with direction. As you know, the role of the leader is yours— it is your job to hold the reins!

The Husky was bred first and foremost to be a working dog, and these working instincts are still a very large part of the dog's personality. Since the average pet Husky owner will not be using his dog for hunting or pulling a sled, the dog needs to have his working energies redirected toward other activities. When not used in a working capacity, the Siberian

A Husky can be happy indoors or out...as long as he has a friend.

Husky must have exercise or else he will be bored. A bored dog will find a way to amuse himself, which could spell trouble for your garden, furniture, shoes, etc. This is not to say that every dog will revert to destructive behavior when he has nothing else to do, but wouldn't you rather be in control of how your dog spends his "free time"? Besides, occupying your dog's time gives you a chance to spend time together, constantly reinforcing the bond you formed when your

Originally intended to be working dogs, Siberian Huskies need an outlet for their energy. Regular walks will provide the pet Husky with some much-needed activity and exercise.

Siberian Husky was just a pup.

While your Husky will adapt to very cold temperatures, excessive heat may bother him. Remember the Arctic climate whence he comes—he's "well-suited" for snow and ice, not for heat and humidity. Keep that in mind and always give your Husky access to shade and fresh water. Never leave your dog in a parked car in warm weather. Dogs of Northern descent have practically no tolerance for heat and will succumb to heat stroke within a very short time.

Siberian Huskies are also well known for being meticu-

Huskies are known for their fierce devotion and loyalty to their owners.

ACTIVITIES TO OCCUPY YOUR HUSKY

Since the Siberian Husky is among the most active dogs, in both mind and body, the owner should be well prepared to keep his dog busy. Here are some popular ways to do so:

1. Daily walks, at least twice a day, for no less than a mile or two.
2. Jogging or cycling.
3. Backpacking.
4. Sledding or skijoring.
5. Camping and hiking.
6. Frisbee or flyball.
7. Carting.
8. Yard work.
9. Weight pulling.
10. Organized dog shows and trials.

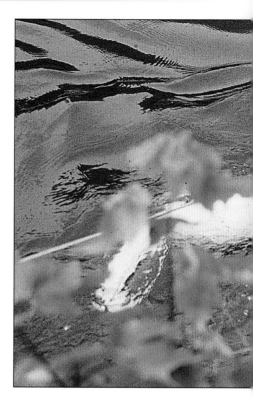

lously clean. Although they shed, this is not a hygiene problem. Instead, the dogs maintain their own cleanliness and have surprisingly little "doggy" smell. They are also easy to groom. Although that thick coat may look intimidating, all they need is brushing; no special grooming is required for the show ring. Keep in mind that the double coat of the Siberian will mat and become very unkempt if not brushed regularly. No matter how fastidious your Husky is, he simply cannot groom his entire coat, especially the parts that he cannot crane his neck to reach.

THE FLIP SIDE OF OWNING A HUSKY

So the Siberian Husky's gregarious personality and gentle manner are just what you're looking for in a dog! You think that the Siberian Husky must be the perfect breed for you. Well, like with most things, there are two sides to the coin. Albeit few, there are negatives to owning a Siberian Husky, so weigh these carefully against the many positives before you make your decision.

First, Siberian Huskies shed. Those thick woolly coats

Although their first love is snow, some Siberian Huskies have an affinity for water as well. Your Husky should only be allowed to go for a swim under your careful supervision.

are beautiful to look at and a joy to snuggle up to, but will you feel the same way when the hair is on your clothes and furniture rather than on your dog? At least once a year, your Husky will shed his coat, so be prepared. Also keep in mind that many people can be allergic to a dog that has as much fur as the Siberian Husky. New owners have discovered, to their dismayed broken heart, that they are sneezing constantly around their Husky even though they were never allergic to the family dogs with whom they grew up as children (a Pug, Poodle or Labrador Retriever).

Second, we know that, in general, dogs like to dig. Huskies, however, *really* like to dig! This habit likely stems from the Husky's instinct to dig a burrow in the ground to keep warm while resting on the snow-covered tundra. Digging in dirt is much better than digging in snow—it's much warmer! If you are willing either to leave your landscaping to chance or to provide your dog with an area of the yard in

A young musher races his team of Huskies in a sled-dog competition held in Pagosa Springs, Colorado.

Regular grooming will rid your Husky's coat of dead hairs and prevent them from ending up on your clothing and furniture.

which to dig, then this should not be a problem. However, if you think this will really bother you and that you will spend most of your time being angry at the dog, then, again, look for another breed.

Third, Siberians run! Fast! If you are looking for a dog to train off-lead for an expedition to the beach or the park, you better choose a different breed. All of the Northern breeds have a propensity to flee. For a Husky, it's a romantic notion: seeking the unattainable, running into the wind, conquering the ends of the earth. Put a leash on your Husky or you may never see

him again. This is a disadvantage, one must admit, for it also means that a dog that likes to run and likes to dig also likes to escape! If you don't have a fenced yard, you have two options: 1. Get a different breed; 2. Get a fence, a good one!

BREED-SPECIFIC HEALTH CONCERNS

The Siberian Husky, not unlike other breeds of pure-bred dog, is prone to a number of hereditary and congenital diseases. Breeders around the world dedicate themselves to minimizing the occurrence of these problems by screening their stock for problems and excluding any affected animals from their breeding programs. Among the two most prominent areas of Siberian health, breeders are concerned with the eyes and hips of the breed. Health concerns are mentioned here not to dissuade the potential Husky owner, but to raise awareness so that the owner can provide his dog with the best possible care.

EYE PROBLEMS

Few could argue that the eyes of the Siberian Husky are one of the breed's most attractive features. It is indeed ironic that the breeders should be concerned about preserving the vision of the exquisite eyes of the Husky. Nonetheless, eye problems are the most prevalent of all disorders in the breed. Potential owners are not to be discouraged by this information. The incidence of problems is indeed low for the breed in general, maybe five percent.

Glaucoma is a buildup of pressure in the dog's eyeball. The eyeball's drainage channel becomes narrow, and eventually blocked, and the increase in pressure can result in blindness. All Siberian Huskies should be tested for glaucoma at one year of age, and if it is indicated that he is predisposed for glaucoma, then he cannot be bred. Dogs that are labeled "predisposed" must be tested annually, and dogs that actually develop glaucoma are labeled "affected."

Hereditary cataracts cause a cloudiness in the eye that can lead to blindness. This can be operated on, but the dog's sight cannot be restored to that of a normal dog. Annual checkups will help detect cataracts, and an affected dog should not be bred. Bilateral cataracts, also known as juvenile cataracts, occur in younger dogs, and are hereditary in the Siberian Husky. In Huskies, the most commonly identified cataracts are found in the posterior axial subcapsular region of the lens. Such cataracts mature as the dog grows old. In certain cases,

The Husky's eyes are perhaps the breed's most beautiful and remarkable feature; unfortunately, eye problems are of major concern in the breed.

the cataract can be detected in one eye before the other eye appears affected. In severe cases, the dog can go blind because of the intensity of the opacities in the eyes.

Corneal dystrophy is a condition that has similar symptoms to those of cataracts in that the dog's eye gets cloudy and his vision becomes blocked. The preferred veterinary term for the condition is crystalline corneal opacities (CCO). This term describes the cone-shaped crystals that are produced in the cornea and that spread across the surface, potentially interfering with the dog's vision. Both eyes are affected by CCO, as in bilateral cataracts, though not simultaneously or to the same degree in every incidence.

Siberian Huskies used as sled dogs must be hardy, healthy dogs with sound hips and clear eyes.

Progressive retinal atrophy (PRA) is a common eye condition that affects most breeds of dogs, and the Husky is not excluded. There are two types of PRA, primary retinal dystrophy and central progressive atrophy. The more common of the two is primary retinal dystrophy, known as night blindness. Night blindness indicates that the dog's sight in the darkness diminishes as the cone cells degenerate. Eventually the dog's day vision is also affected. At the early stages it may seem that only one eye is affected, but in actuality both eyes are affected in every incidence. As the term "progressive" indicates, the disease worsens as time goes on, eventually leading to total blindness. Although PRA is inherited in the Siberian Husky, the incidence is so minor that there is no conclusive evidence on its heritability.

HIP DYSPLASIA

Canine hip dysplasia, the most common orthopedic problem in dogs, refers to the abnormal development of the hip joint. All dogs with hip dysplasia (HD) are born with normal hips, which eventually deteriorate by the time the dog is two years old. In dysplastic dogs, the femur (thigh bone) does not properly fit into the acetabulum (pelvic joint socket).

Since the Siberian Husky is bred as a drafting sled dog, its ability to run with strength and stamina is tantamount to its reason for living. Considering that hip dysplasia prohibits a Husky's being able to do the job that it was bred to do, breeders place much emphasis on eliminating HD from the breed. The occurrence of HD in the Husky is estimated to be approximately 4 to 5 percent, which is considerably low compared to some other larger breeds whose incidence can be as high as 40 to 50 percent.

Through the Orthopedic Foundation for Animals (OFA), Huskies screened for HD can generate seven kinds of results: 1. Excellent; 2. Good; 3. Fair; 4. Borderline; 5. Mild; 6. Moderate; and 7. Severe. Most Huskies receive excellent scores with only about 1% of the population considered dysplastic. Only dogs free of HD should be included in breeding programs. This can be a heartbreaking scenario for the breeder who has an otherwise flawless champion who scores poorly. Not all dogs who are tested for HD will show signs of degeneration. These dogs nonetheless are carriers and can pass the disease to their progeny. Potential owners should inquire about the puppies' parents and grandparents and other close relatives. Since the mode of

Your Siberian Husky should have a vet who can monitor its health on a regular basis. This young Husky is getting a vaccination.

(FACING PAGE) Husky pups can inherit beautiful markings, but, unfortunately, they can also inherit health problems. Knowing a lot about your dog's lineage can be very helpful in evaluating its future health.

inheritance is not fully understood, careful discretion is well advised.

In addition to excluding dysplastic dogs from breeding programs, breeders also take other precautions to ensure that HD does not creep into their lines. Environmental factors concern breeders as do the hereditary ones. Providing newborn puppies

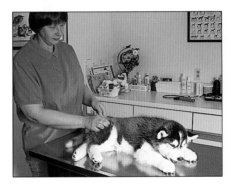

with non-slip surfaces in the whelping boxes prevents awkward puppies from injuring their fragile bones and ligaments. Likewise, breeders recommend diets free from supplements and low in fats to avoid puppies' gaining more weight than their growing frames can support. Owners of young puppies should also limit the kinds of exercise that their puppies receive. Unsupervised roughhousing and jumping should be excluded from the exercise regimen as it can cause damage to the Husky's growing bones and joints.

The American Kennel Club's breed standards are very clear and detailed. The goal is to outline the desired characteristics of each breed in order to preserve the uniformity, in both physical attributes and personality, of each dog breed. A champion-quality dog must possess all of these characteristics.

BREED STANDARD FOR THE

SIBERIAN HUSKY

WHAT IS A STANDARD?

A breed standard is the blue-print of the dog, a written description of what breeders and judges are looking for in a perfect example of a Siberian Husky. Breeders use the standard as a guideline, a set of goals for which to strive. Judges use the standard to evaluate how well the breeders are doing in reaching that goal of a perfect dog. If you are planning to show your dog, use this standard as a barometer to determine how well your maturing puppy compares to the ideal set forth herein. Since the Siberian Husky is a slow-developing breed, do not expect that your four-month-old puppy is going to mirror the standard perfectly. Some breed representatives do not fully mature until three years of age, although your Husky should begin shaping up by 12 to 16 months.

The following standard is excerpted from the one recognized by the American Kennel Club, America's main dog-regulating body. Since the Husky is popular all around the world, there are several different standards, sometimes even within the same country. These standards vary slightly in wording and detail, though each essentially describes the dog we recognize as the Siberian Husky.

If your Husky puppy develops into a handsome adult, why not try your hand at conformation showing?

THE AMERICAN KENNEL CLUB STANDARD FOR THE SIBERIAN HUSKY

General Appearance: The Siberian Husky is a medium-sized working dog, quick and light on his feet and free and graceful in action. His moderately compact and well furred body, erect ears and brush tail suggest his Northern heritage. His characteristic gait is smooth and seemingly effortless. He performs his original function in harness most capably, carrying a light load at a moderate speed over great distances. His body proportions and form reflect this basic balance of power, speed and endurance. The males of the Siberian Husky breed are masculine but never coarse; the bitches are feminine but without weakness of structure. In proper condition, with muscle firm and well developed, the Siberian Husky does not carry excess weight.

Size, Proportion, Substance: *Height*—Dogs, 21 to 23.5 inches at

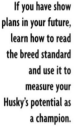

If you have show plans in your future, learn how to read the breed standard and use it to measure your Husky's potential as a champion.

the withers. Bitches, 20 to 22 inches at the withers. **Weight**—Dogs, 45 to 60 pounds. Bitches, 35 to 50 pounds. Weight is in proportion to height. The measurements mentioned above represent the extreme height and weight limits with no preference given to either extreme. Any appearance of excessive bone or weight should be penalized. In profile, the length of the body from the point of the shoulder to the rear point of the croup is slightly longer than the height of the body from the ground to the top of the withers. *Disqualification—Dogs over 23.5 inches and bitches over 22 inches.*

Head: Expression is keen, but friendly; interested and even mischievous. Eyes almond shaped, moderately spaced and set a trifle obliquely. Eyes may be brown or blue in color; one of each or parti-colored are acceptable. *Faults— Eyes set too obliquely; set too close together.* Ears of medium size, triangular in shape, close fitting and set high on the head. They are thick, well furred, slightly arched at the back, and strongly erect, with slightly rounded tips pointing straight up. *Faults—Ears too large in proportion to the head; too wide set; not strongly erect.* Skull of medium size and in proportion to the body; slightly rounded on top and tapering from the widest point to the eyes. *Faults—Head clumsy or heavy; head too finely chiseled.*

Stop—The stop is well-defined and the bridge of the nose is straight from the stop to the tip. *Fault— Insufficient stop.* Muzzle of medium length; that is, the distance from the tip of the nose to the stop is equal to the distance from the stop to the occiput. The muzzle is of medium width, tapering gradually to the nose, with the tip neither pointed nor square. *Faults—Muzzle either too snipy or too coarse; muzzle too short or too long.* Nose black in gray, tan or

An exceptionally fine Husky in a striking color. The overall appearance of the dog should be alert and graceful.

black dogs; liver in copper dogs; may be flesh-colored in pure white dogs. The pink-streaked "snow nose" is acceptable. Lips are well pigmented and close fitting. Teeth closing in a scissors bite. *Fault— Any bite other than scissors.*

Neck, Topline, Body: Neck medium in length, arched and carried proudly erect when dog is standing. When moving at a trot,

The Husky's ears should be triangular in shape and relatively close together.

The forequarters should demonstrate well laid back shoulder blades. The forelegs should be moderately spaced, parallel to each other and straight.

from the spine at an angle, but never so steeply as to restrict the rearward thrust of the hind legs. *Faults—Weak or slack back; roached back; sloping topline.*

Tail: The well furred tail of fox-brush shape is set on just below the level of the topline, and is usually carried over the back in a graceful sickle curve when the dog is at attention. When carried up, the tail does not curl to either side of the body, nor does it snap flat against the back. A trailing tail is normal for the dog when in repose. Hair on

the neck is extended so that the head is carried slightly forward. *Faults—Neck too short and thick; neck too long.* Chest deep and strong, but not too broad, with the deepest point being just behind and level with the elbows. The ribs are well sprung from the spine but flattened on the sides to allow for freedom of action. *Faults—Chest too broad; "barrel ribs"; ribs too flat or weak.* **Back**—The back is straight and strong, with a level topline from withers to croup. It is of medium length, neither cobby nor slack from excessive length. The loin is taut and lean, narrower than the rib cage, and with a slight tuck-up. The croup slopes away

the tail is of medium length and approximately the same length on top, sides and bottom, giving the appearance of a round brush. *Faults—A snapped or tightly curled tail; highly plumed tail; tail set too low or too high.*

Forequarters: *Shoulders*—The shoulder blade is well laid back. The upper arm angles slightly backward from point of shoulder to elbow, and is never perpendicular to the ground. The muscles and

The teeth should form a scissors bite with the upper teeth closely overlapping the lower teeth.

The Husky's body should be straight and strong, with a level topline.

EARS
High on head and close fitting (left). Ears on right are too far apart and not held correctly.

FOREQUARTERS
Forelegs parallel and straight (left), turning neither in nor out (right).

TAIL
Well furred, should be held up in sickle curve (left), not curled too tightly (right).

FEET
Oval and compact (left); thickly padded and well furred between toes (right).

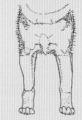 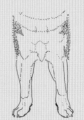

GAIT
Smooth and effortless; topline remains level; reach and drive in legs is evident.

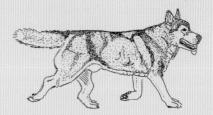

Although the breed
standard was written with
function in mind, the
Siberian Husky is a dog that
possesses remarkable
natural beauty as well.

ligaments holding the shoulder to the rib cage are firm and well developed. *Faults—Straight shoulders; loose shoulders.*

Forelegs—When standing and viewed from the front, the legs are moderately spaced, parallel and straight, with the elbows close to the body and turned neither in nor out. Viewed from the side, pasterns are slightly slanted, with the pastern joint strong, but flexible. Bone is substantial but never heavy. Length of the leg from elbow to ground is slightly more than the

distance from the elbow to the top of withers. Dewclaws on forelegs may be removed. *Faults—Weak pasterns; too heavy bone; too narrow or too wide in the front; out at the elbows.* Feet oval in shape but not long. The paws are medium in size, compact and well furred between the toes and pads. The pads are tough and thickly cushioned. The paws neither turn in nor out when the dog is in natural stance. *Faults—Soft or splayed toes; paws too large and clumsy; paws too small and delicate; toeing in or out.*

Hindquarters: When standing and viewed from the rear, the hind legs are moderately spaced and parallel. The upper thighs are well muscled and powerful, the stifles well bent, the hock joint well-defined and set low to the ground. Dewclaws, if any, are to be removed. *Faults—Straight stifles, cow-hocks, too narrow or too wide in the rear.*

Coat: The coat of the Siberian Husky is double and medium in length, giving a well furred appear-

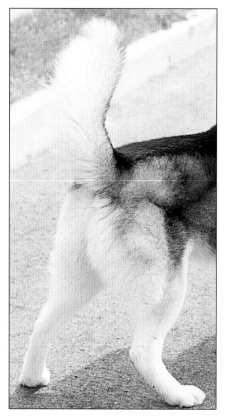

ance, but is never so long as to obscure the clean-cut outline of the dog. The undercoat is soft and dense and of sufficient length to support the outer coat. The guard hairs of the outer coat are straight and somewhat smooth lying, never harsh nor standing straight off from the body. It should be noted that the absence of the undercoat during the shedding season is normal. Trimming of whiskers and fur between the toes and around the feet to present a neater appearance is permissible. Trimming the fur on any other part of the dog is not to be condoned and should be severely penalized. *Faults—Long, rough, or shaggy coat; texture too harsh or too silky; trimming of the coat, except as permitted above.*

Color: All colors from black to pure white are allowed. A variety of markings on the head is common, including many striking patterns not found in other breeds.

Gait: The Siberian Husky's characteristic gait is smooth and seemingly effortless. He is quick and light on his feet, and when in the show ring should be gaited on a loose lead at a moderately fast trot, exhibiting good reach in the forequarters and good drive in the hindquarters. When viewed from the front to rear while moving at a walk the Siberian Husky does not single-track, but as the speed increases the legs gradually angle inward until the pads are falling on a line directly under the longitudinal center of the body. As the pad marks converge, the forelegs and hind legs are carried straightforward, with neither elbows nor stifles turned in or out. Each hind

This working Husky demonstrates a keen expression, thick double coat and tail held up in a graceful curve.

leg moves in the path of the foreleg on the same side. While the dog is gaiting, the topline remains firm and level. *Faults—Short, prancing or choppy gait, lumbering or rolling gait; crossing or crabbing.*

Temperament: The characteristic temperament of the Siberian Husky is friendly and gentle, but also alert and outgoing. He does not display the possessive qualities of the guard dog, nor is he overly suspicious of strangers or aggressive with other dogs. Some measure of reserve and dignity may be expected in the mature dog. His intelligence, tractability, and eager disposition make him an agreeable companion and willing worker.

SIBERIAN HUSKY

SELECTING A BREEDER AND PUPPY

Beholding a litter of Siberian Husky puppies can be an overwhelming experience. All puppies are cute, but furry puppies have an ineffable appeal that can make human beings do foolish things. The author is here to help you keep your wits as you encounter a litter of Siberian Husky pups and make a well-informed choice. Even a litter of poorly bred, unsocialized, undernourished Siberian Huskies is cute, to an extent. An educated

YOUR SCHEDULE . . .
If you lead an erratic, unpredictable life, with daily or weekly changes in your work requirements, consider the problems of owning a puppy. The new puppy has to be fed regularly, socialized (loved, petted, handled, introduced to other people) and, most importantly, allowed to go outdoors for house-training. As the dog gets older, it can be more tolerant of deviations in its feeding and relief schedule.

(FACING PAGE)
You should always try to meet at least one of the parents of your prospective puppy. Looks, personality and soundness are inherited.

eye will appreciate the added appeal of a well-bred, well-fed, well-loved litter.

Selecting a breeder for your Siberian Husky should be relatively easy. You are looking for an established breeder with outstanding dog ethics and a strong commitment to the breed. Why? Why not just find a litter in the local newspaper and call that breeder? Wouldn't that be more *convenient*?

New owners should have as many questions as they have doubts. An established breeder is indeed the one to answer your seven thousand questions and to allay your doubts about

Husky puppies are cute, but that's not enough reason to bring a pup home. Read this chapter carefully before you select your Husky puppy.

Husky puppies are adorable...don't be surprised if you fall in love with the entire litter!

ownership. An established breeder will sell you a puppy, at a fair price, if, and only if, the breeder determines that you are a suitable, worthy owner of his/her dogs. An established breeder can be relied upon for advice, no matter what time of day or night. A reputable breeder will accept a puppy back, without questions, should you decide that this is not the right dog for you.

Owning a dog is not really a convenience, so convenience doesn't play a part, as responsibility and commitment do. It's not convenient to have a four-legged wolf-creature crawling around your house, chewing, piddling and messing every room it enters. We don't choose to share our homes with dogs because it's *convenient!* But there are other fringe benefits to this thing we call dog ownership.

That local breeder, trying so hard to get rid of that first litter of ten puppies, is more than accommodating and anxious to sell you a puppy. That local breeder lives only a couple of miles away. That local breeder isn't going to interrogate you and your family about your intentions with their puppy, the environment and training you can provide, etc. Unlike the knowledgeable breeder, who has his dogs screened for hip and eye defects (e.g., hip dysplasia, cataracts, PRA, etc.), that local breeder can't even spell *ophthalmologist!* That local breeder will be nowhere to be found when your poorly bred, badly adjusted four-pawed monster starts to growl and spit up at midnight.

Choosing a breeder is an important first step in dog ownership. There is no doubt. Fortunately, the majority of Siberian Husky breeders is devoted to the breed and its well-being. New owners should have little problem finding a reputable breeder who doesn't live in a different state or on the other

PUPPY APPEARANCE
Your puppy should have a well-fed appearance but not a distended abdomen, which may indicate worms or incorrect feeding, or both. The body should be firm, with a solid feel. The skin of the abdomen should be pale pink and clean, without signs of scratching or rash. Dewclaws may be removed; check to see if the breeder has had this done.

side of the country. The American Kennel Club is able to refer you to breeders of quality Siberian Huskies, as could any local all-breed club or Husky club. Potential owners are encouraged to attend a dog show to see the Huskies in action, to meet the breeders and handlers firsthand and to get an idea what Huskies look like outside a photographer's lens. Provided you approach the owners when they are not engaged in grooming or handling the dogs, most are more than willing to answer questions, recommend breeders and give advice.

Once you have contacted and met a breeder or two and made your choice about which breeder is best suited toward your needs, it's time to visit the litter. Whoa! (that's a musher's term that means slow down). Keep in mind, O, anxious Husky owner,

PEDIGREE VS. REGISTRATION CERTIFICATE

Too often new owners are confused between these two important documents. Your puppy's pedigree, essentially a family tree, is a written record of a dog's genealogy of three generations or more. The pedigree will show you the names as well as performance titles of all the dogs in your pup's background. Your breeder must provide you with a registration application, with his part properly filled out. You must complete the application and send it to the AKC with the proper fee. Every puppy must come from a litter that has been AKC-registered by the breeder, born in the USA and from sire and dam that are also registered with the AKC.

The seller must provide you with complete records to identify the puppy. The AKC requires that the seller provide the buyer with the following: breed; sex, color and markings; date of birth; litter number (when available); names and registration numbers of the parents; breeder's name; and date sold or delivered.

No matter how hard it is to resist, do not buy the first Husky puppy that you see. Shop around and compare until you find the perfect match.

that many top breeders have waiting lists. Sometimes new owners have to wait as long as two years for a puppy. If you are really committed to the breeder you've selected, then you will wait (and hope for an early arrival!). If not, you may have to resort to your second- or third-choice breeder. Don't be too anxious, however. If the breeder

The Husky's beautiful markings are evident even in very young puppies.

doesn't have any waiting list, or any customers, there is probably a good reason. It's no different than visiting a restaurant with no customers. The better restaurants always have a waiting list—and it's usually worth the wait. Besides, isn't a dog more important than a fine meal?

When viewing a litter of Siberian Husky puppies, you are looking for friendly, outgoing pups. That hopefully describes the whole litter, although there is usually one shy pup who cannot compete with the rest. Huskies are surely pack animals, and the pecking order in the pack begins to take hold by the time the pups are four or five weeks of age. Breeders commonly allow visitors to see the litter by around the fifth or sixth week, and puppies leave for their new homes between the eighth and tenth week. Breeders who permit their puppies to leave early are more interested in your money than their puppies' well-being. Puppies need to learn the rules of the trade from their dams, and most dams continue teaching the pups manners and "dos and

don'ts" until around the eighth week. Breeders actively socialize the puppies so that they are able to interact with the "other species," i.e., humans! Given the long history that dogs and humans have, bonding between the two species is natural but must be nurtured. With Siberian Huskies, the bond is even more evident, considering the customs of the Chukchis' raising puppies with children. A well-bred, well-socialized Husky pup wants nothing more than to be near you and please you. That's as *convenient* as a puppy can be!

What other considerations might an owner entertain in choosing a pup? Most breeders agree that the sex of the puppy is immaterial. Some people believe that females are more affectionate and males more aloof. Others will tell you that the male, especially

ARE YOU A FIT OWNER?

If the breeder from whom you are buying a puppy asks you a lot of personal questions, do not be insulted. Such a breeder wants to be sure that you will be a fit provider for his puppy.

COMMITMENT OF OWNERSHIP

After considering all of these factors, you have most likely already made some very important decisions about selecting your puppy. You have chosen a Siberian Husky, which means the unaltered male, will wander away from home in search of females in heat. With the Husky, this should not pertain, since both the males and the females will wander away if given the opportunity. The color of the Husky puppy is also not important, and the patterns in the breed can be quite dramatic. Certainly the pattern will change and develop as the puppy grows. You may also find a puppy that is solid white—this is just as acceptable as any other combination of colors. Many breeders recommend that owners consider an older puppy, say four to six months of age. Often breeders hold on to puppies to evaluate their showing and breeding potential and then release them if they do not quite make the grade. Such a puppy is usually wonderfully socialized, house-trained and as handsome as a pet could be.

ARE YOU PREPARED?

Unfortunately, when a puppy is bought by someone who does not take into consideration the time and attention that dog ownership requires, it is the puppy who suffers when he is either abandoned or placed in a shelter by a frustrated owner. So all of the "homework" you do in preparation for your pup's arrival will benefit you both. The more informed you are, the more you will know what to expect and the better equipped you will be to handle the ups and downs of raising a puppy. Hopefully, everyone in the household is willing to do his part in raising and caring for the pup. The anticipation of owning a dog often brings a lot of promises from excited family members: "I will walk him every day," "I will feed him," "I will house-train him," etc., but these things take time and effort, and promises can easily be forgotten once the novelty of the new pet has worn off.

that you have decided which characteristics you want in a dog and what type of dog will best fit into your family and lifestyle. If you have selected a breeder, you have gone a step further—you have done your research and found a responsible, conscientious person who breeds quality Siberian Huskies and who should become a reliable source of help as you and your puppy adjust to life together. If you have observed a litter in action, you have obtained a firsthand look at the dynamics of a puppy "pack" and, thus, you have gotten to learn about each pup's individual personality—perhaps you have even found one that particularly appeals to you.

However, even if you have not yet found the Siberian Husky puppy of your dreams, observing pups will help you learn to recognize certain behavior and to determine what a pup's behavior indicates about his temperament. You will be able to pick out which pups are the leaders, which ones are less outgoing, which ones are confident, which ones are shy, playful, friendly, aggressive, etc. Equally as

> **BOY OR GIRL?**
> An important consideration to be discussed is the sex of your puppy. For a family companion, a bitch may be the better choice, considering the female's inbred concern for all young creatures and her accompanying tolerance and patience. It is always advisable to spay a pet bitch, which may guarantee her a longer life.

important, you will learn to recognize what a healthy pup should look and act like. All of these things will help you in your search, and when you find the Siberian Husky that was meant for you, you will know it!

Researching your breed, selecting a responsible breeder and observing as many pups as possible are all

This handsome pair shares an almost identical marking pattern.

Siberian Huskies are known for being one of the friendliest breeds around. If you need convincing, just look at these happy pups!

important steps on the way to dog ownership. It may seem like a lot of effort...and you have not even taken the pup home yet! Remember, though, you

PET INSURANCE

Just like you can insure your car, your house and your own health, you likewise can insure your dog's health. Investigate a pet insurance policy by talking to your vet. Depending on the age of your dog, the breed and the kind of coverage you desire, your policy can be very affordable. Most policies cover accidental injuries, poisoning, and thousands of medical problems and illnesses. Some carriers also offer routine care and immunization coverage, including spaying/neutering, health screening and more.

cannot be too careful when it comes to deciding on the type of dog you want and finding out about your prospective pup's background. Buying a puppy is not—or should not be—just another whimsical purchase. In fact, this is one instance in which you actually do get to choose your own family! But, you may be thinking, buying a puppy should be fun—it should not be so serious and so much work. If you keep in mind the thought that your puppy is not a cuddly stuffed toy or decorative lawn ornament, but instead will become a real member of your family, you will realize that while buying a puppy is a pleasurable and exciting endeavor, it is not something to be taken lightly. Relax...the fun will start when the pup comes home!

They may look like cuddly toys, but puppies are living creatures that need attention, love and care.

Always keep in mind that a puppy is nothing more than a baby in a furry disguise...a baby who is virtually helpless in a human world and who trusts his owner for fulfillment of his basic needs for survival. That goes beyond food, water and shelter; your pup needs care, protection, guidance and love. If you are not prepared to commit to this, then you are not prepared to own a dog.

"Wait a minute," you say. "How hard could this be? All of my neighbors own dogs and they seem to be doing just fine. Why should I have to worry about all of this?" Well, you should not worry about it; in fact, you will probably find that once your Siberian Husky pup gets used to his new home, he will fall into his place in the family quite naturally. But it never hurts to emphasize the commitment of dog ownership. With some time and patience, it is really not too difficult to raise a curious and exuberant Siberian Husky pup to

be a well-adjusted and well-mannered adult dog—a dog that could be your most loyal friend.

PREPARING PUPPY'S PLACE IN YOUR HOME

Researching your breed and finding a breeder are only two aspects of the "homework" you will have to do before bringing your Siberian Husky puppy home. You will also have to prepare your home and family for the new addition. Much like you would prepare a nursery for a newborn baby, you will need to designate a place in your home that will be the puppy's own. How you prepare your home will depend on how much freedom the dog will be allowed: will he be confined to one room or a specific area in the house, or will he be allowed to roam as he pleases? Will he spend most of his time in the house or will he be primarily an outdoor dog? Whatever you decide, you must ensure that he has a place that he can "call his own."

When you bring your new

A HEALTHY PUP
You should not even think about buying a puppy that looks sick, undernourished, overly frightened or nervous. Sometimes a timid puppy will warm up to you after a 30-minute "let's-get-acquainted" session.

TEMPERAMENT COUNTS

Your selection of a good puppy can be determined by your needs. A show potential or a good pet? It is your choice. Every puppy, however, should be of good temperament. Although show-quality puppies are bred and raised with emphasis on physical conformation, responsible breeders strive for equally good temperament. Do not buy from a breeder who concentrates solely on physical beauty at the expense of personality.

puppy into your home, you are bringing him into what will become his home as well. Obviously, you did not buy a puppy so that he could take over your house, but in order for a puppy to grow into a stable, well-adjusted dog, he has to feel comfortable in his surroundings. Remember, he is leaving the warmth and security of his mother and littermates, plus the familiarity of the only place he has ever known, so it is important to make his transition as easy as possible. By preparing a place in your home for the puppy, you are making him feel as welcome as possible in a

A family portrait. The dam's beauty and good temperament was passed on to her litter.

strange new place. It should not take him long to get used to it, but the sudden shock of being transplanted is somewhat traumatic for a young pup. Imagine how a small child would feel in the same situation—that is how your puppy must be feeling. It is up to you to reassure him and to let him know, "Little fellow, you are going to like it here!"

WHAT YOU SHOULD BUY

CRATE

To someone unfamiliar with the use of crates in dog training, it may seem like punishment to shut a dog in a crate; this is not the case at all. Crates are not cruel—crates have many humane and highly effective uses in dog

A TIME TO GO HOME
Breeders rarely release puppies until they are eight to ten weeks of age. This is an acceptable age for most breeds of dog, excepting toy breeds, which are not released until around 12 weeks, given their petite sizes. If a breeder has a puppy that is 12 weeks of age or older, it is likely well socialized and house-trained. Be sure that it is otherwise healthy before deciding to take it home.

care and training. For example, crate training is a very popular and very successful housebreaking method, a crate can keep your dog safe during travel, and, perhaps most importantly, a crate provides your dog with a place of his own in your home. It serves as a "doggie bedroom" of sorts—your Siberian Husky can curl up in his crate when he wants to sleep or when he just needs a break. Many dogs sleep in their crates overnight. When lined with soft blankets and a favorite toy, a crate becomes a cozy pseudo-den for your dog. Like his burrowing ancestors, he too will seek out the comfort and retreat of a den—you just happen to be providing

Observe a litter and you will see "pack mentality" in action.

Fiberglass, as shown here, crates are popular for use while traveling with your dog.

The size of the crate is another thing to consider. Puppies do not stay puppies forever—in fact, sometimes it seems as if they grow right before your eyes. The small-sized crate may be fine for a very young Siberian Husky pup, but it will not do him much good for long! Unless you have the money and the inclination to buy a new crate every time your pup has a growth spurt, it is better to get one that

him with something a little more luxurious than leaves and twigs lining a dirty ditch.

As far as purchasing a crate, there are two popular types: wire or fiberglass. There are advantages and disadvantages to each type. For example, a wire crate is more open, allowing the air to flow through and affording the dog a view of what is going on around him. Given the nature of Siberian Huskies, the wire crate is the preferred type for around the house. Huskies like to see what's going on around them and will not accept the "confinement" of a fiberglass crate. A fiberglass crate is sturdier than the wire crate and is a requirement for air or rail travel.

A CRATE TO CALL HIS OWN

During crate training, you should partition off the section of the crate in which the pup stays. If he is given too big an area, this will hinder your training efforts. Crate training is based on the fact that a dog does not like to soil his sleeping quarters, so it is ineffective to keep a pup in a crate that is so big that he can eliminate in one end and get far enough away from it to sleep. Also, you want to make the crate den-like for the pup. Blankets and a favorite toy will make the crate cozy for the small pup; as he grows, you may want to evict some of his "roommates" to make more room. It will take some coaxing at first, but be patient. Given some time to get used to it, your pup will adapt to his new home-within-a-home quite nicely.

will accommodate your dog both as a pup and at full size. A large crate will be necessary for a full-grown Siberian Husky, as their approximate weight range is between 35 and 60 pounds.

BEDDING

A nice crate pad and a soft blanket in the dog's crate will help the dog feel more at home. First, the pad will take the place of the leaves, twigs, etc., that the pup would use in the wild to make a den; the pup can make his own "burrow" in the crate. Although your pup is somewhat removed from his den-making ancestors, the denning instinct is very much a part of his genetic makeup. Second, until you bring your pup home, he has been sleeping amid the warmth of his mother and littermates, and while a blanket is not the same as a warm, breathing body, it still provides heat and something with which to snuggle. You will want to wash your pup's blanket

PHOTO COURTESY OF DOSKOCIL.

frequently in case he has an accident in his crate, and replace or remove any blanket that becomes ragged and starts to fall apart.

TOYS

Toys are a must for dogs of all ages, especially for curious playful pups. Puppies are the "children" of the dog world, and what child does not love toys? Chew toys provide enjoyment to both dog and owner—your dog will enjoy

Left: Acclimating your Husky to a crate will be one of the most important things that you do in training your dog.

More than one Husky means more than one crate! Whether traveling a long distance or just around the corner, your dog should always be kept secure in his crate—but please, only one dog per crate.

PUPPY PROBLEMS

The majority of problems that are commonly seen in young pups will disappear as your dog gets older. However, how you deal with problems when he is young will determine how he reacts to discipline as an adult dog. It is important to establish who is boss (hopefully it will be you!) right away when you are first bonding with your dog. This bond will set the tone for the rest of your life together.

everything looks appetizing! The full range of your possessions—from old hand towels to Oriental carpet—are fair game in the eyes of a teething pup. Puppies are not all that discerning when it comes to finding something to literally "sink their teeth into"—everything tastes great!

Stuffed toys are another option; these are good to put in the dog's crate to give him some company. Be careful of these, as a pup can de-stuff one pretty quickly, and stay away from stuffed toys with small plastic eyes or parts that a pup could choke on. Similarly, squeaky toys are quite popular. There are dogs that will come running from anywhere in the house at the first sound from their favorite squeaky friend. Again, if a pup de-stuffs one of these, the small plastic squeaker inside can be dangerous if swallowed. Monitor the condition of your pup's toys carefully and get rid of any that have been chewed to the point of becoming potentially dangerous.

playing with his favorite toys, while you will enjoy the fact that they distract him from your expensive shoes and leather couch. Puppies love to chew; in fact, chewing is a physical need for pups as they are teething and

Be careful of natural bones, which have a tendency to splinter into sharp, dangerous pieces. Also be careful of rawhide, which after enough chewing can turn into pieces that are easy to swallow, and also watch out for the mushy mess it can turn into on your carpet.

Your Husky should have a toy in his crate to help him feel comfortable and keep him occupied.

LEAD

A nylon lead is probably the best option as it is the most resistant to puppy teeth should your pup take a liking to chewing on his lead. Of course, this is a habit that should be nipped in the bud, but if your pup likes to chew on his lead he has a very slim chance of being able to chew through the strong nylon. Nylon leads are also lightweight, which is good for a young Siberian Husky who is just getting used to the idea of walking on a lead. For everyday walking and safety purposes, the nylon lead is a good choice. As your pup grows up and gets used to walking on the lead, and can do it politely,

TOYS, TOYS, TOYS!

With a big variety of dog toys available, and so many that look like they would be a lot of fun for a dog, be careful in your selection. It is amazing what a set of puppy teeth can do to an innocent-looking toy, so, obviously, safety is a major consideration. Be sure to choose the most durable products that you can find. Hard nylon bones and toys are a safe bet and many of them are offered in different scents and flavors that will be sure to capture your dog's attention. It is always fun to play a game of catch with your dog and there are balls and flying discs that are specially made to withstand dog teeth.

Pet shops have a large selection of safe, durable pet toys suitable for training and entertaining your Siberian Husky.

IN DUE TIME
It will take at least two weeks for your puppy to become accustomed to his new surroundings. Give him lots of love, attention, handling, frequent opportunities to relieve himself, a diet he likes to eat and a place he can call his own.

Your local pet shop should have a large assortment of collars and leads from which you can make a selection according to the size of your dog and your budget.

you may want to purchase a flexible lead, which allows you either to extend the length to give the dog a broader area to explore or to pull in the lead when you want to keep him close. Of course there are special leads for training purposes, and specially made leather harnesses for the sled-dog Siberian Husky, but these are not necessary for routine walks. If your Siberian Husky is especially strong or tends to pull on the lead, you may want to purchase something stronger, like a thick leather lead.

COLLAR
Your pup should get used to wearing a collar all the time since you will want to attach his ID tags to his collar. Also, the lead and collar go hand in hand—you

have to attach the lead to something! A lightweight nylon collar will be a good choice; make sure that it fits snugly enough so that the pup cannot wriggle out of it, but loose enough so that it will not be uncomfortably tight around the pup's neck. You should be able to fit a finger in between the pup and the collar. It may take some time for your pup to get used to wearing the collar, but soon he will not even notice that it is there. Choke collars are made for training, but should only be used by an owner who knows exactly how to use it. If you use a stronger leather lead or a chain lead to

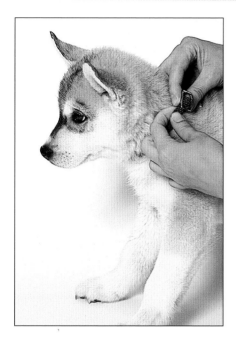

walk your Siberian Husky, you will need a stronger collar as well.

FOOD AND WATER BOWLS

Your pup will need two bowls, one for food and one for water. You may want two sets of bowls, one for inside and one for outside, depending on where the dog will be fed and where he will be spending most of his time. Stainless steel or sturdy plastic bowls are popular choices. Although plastic bowls are more chewable, dogs tend not to chew on the steel variety, which can also be sterilized. Some dog owners like to put their dogs' food and water bowls on specially made elevated stands; this brings the food closer to the dog's

level so he does not have to crane his neck while eating, thus aiding his digestion and helping to guard against bloat or gastric torsion in deep-chested dogs. The most important thing is to buy sturdy bowls since, again, anything is in danger of being chewed by puppy teeth and you do not want your dog to be constantly chewing apart his bowl (for his safety and for your wallet!).

CLEANING SUPPLIES

A pup that is not house-trained means you will be doing a lot of cleaning until he is. Accidents will occur, which is okay for now because he does not know any better. All you can do is clean up any "accidents"—old rags, paper towels, newspapers and a safe disinfectant are good to have on hand.

BEYOND THE BASICS

The items previously discussed are the bare necessities. You will find out what else you need as

Your first purchase of a collar should be a buckle collar to which you can attach the dog's identification tags.

PHOTO COURTESY OF MIKKI PET PRODUCTS.

Dog dishes and bowls are manufactured from plastic, pottery and stainless steel.

Pet shops offer a wide range of food and water bowls. Consider buying two sets...one for inside and one for outside.

you go along—grooming supplies, flea/tick protection, baby gates to partition a room, etc.—these things will vary depending on your situation. It is just important that right away you have everything you need to feed and make your Siberian Husky comfortable in his first few days at home.

PUPPY-PROOFING YOUR HOME

Aside from making sure that your Siberian Husky will be comfortable in your home, you also have to make sure that your home is safe for your Siberian Husky. This means taking precautions to make sure that your pup will not get into anything he should not get into and that there is nothing within his reach that may harm him should he sniff it, chew it, inspect it, etc. This probably seems obvious since, while you are primarily concerned with your pup's safety, at the same time you do not want your belongings to be ruined.

Breakables should be placed out of reach if your dog is to have full run of the house. If he is to be limited to certain places within the house, keep any potentially dangerous items in the "off-limits" areas. An electrical cord can pose a danger should the puppy decide to taste it—and who is going to convince

a pup that it would not make a great chew toy? Cords should be fastened tightly against the wall. If your dog is going to spend time in a crate, make sure that there is nothing near his crate that he can reach if he sticks his curious little nose or paws through the openings. And just as you would with a child, keep all household cleaners and chemicals where the pup cannot get to them.

It is just as important to make sure that the outside of your home is safe. Of course your puppy should never be unsuper-vised, but a pup let loose in the yard will want to run and explore, and he should be granted that freedom. Do not let a fence give you a false sense of security; you would be surprised how crafty (and persistent) a dog can be in figuring out how to dig under and squeeze his way through small holes, or to jump or climb over a fence. The remedy is to make the fence high enough so that it really is impossible for your dog to get over it (at least 6 feet), and well embedded into the ground. Remember that Huskies are dedicated diggers who have a penchant for escaping and running! Be sure to repair or secure any gaps in the fence. Check the fence periodically to ensure that it is in good shape and make repairs as needed; a very determined pup may return

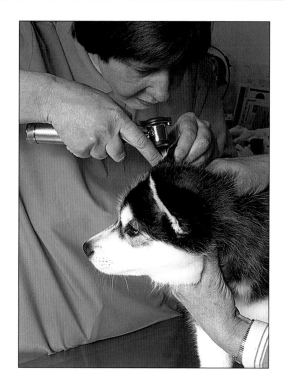

to the same spot to "work on it" until he is able to get through.

FIRST TRIP TO THE VET
Okay, you have picked out your puppy, your home and family are ready, now all you have to do is pick your Siberian Husky up from the breeder and the fun begins, right? Well...not so fast. Something else you need to prepare for is your pup's first trip to the veterinarian. Perhaps the breeder can recommend someone in the area who specializes in Siberian Huskies, or maybe you know some other Siberian Husky owners who can suggest a good

Have your new Husky puppy evaluated by your chosen veterinarian.

vet. Either way, you should have an appointment arranged for your pup before you pick him up; plan on taking him for a check-up within the first few days of bringing him home.

The pup's first visit will consist of an overall examination to make sure that the pup does not have any problems that are not apparent to you. The veterinarian will also set up a schedule for the pup's vaccinations; the breeder will inform you of which ones the pup has already received and the vet can continue from there.

INTRODUCTION TO THE FAMILY

Everyone in the house will be excited about the puppy's coming home and will want to pet him and play with him, but it is best to make the introduction low-key so as not to overwhelm the puppy. He is apprehensive already; it is the first time he has been separated from his mother and the breeder, and the ride to your home is likely the first time he has been in a car. The last thing you want to do is smother him, as this will only frighten him further. This is not to say that human contact is not extremely necessary at this stage, because this is the time when an instant connection between the pup and his human family is formed. Gentle petting

DON'T FENCE ME IN!
The electrical fencing system, which forms an invisible fence, works on a battery-operated collar that shocks the dog if it gets too close to the buried (or elevated) wire. Many experts recommend and think very highly of this system of controlling a dog's wandering. Keep in mind that the collar has batteries. For safety's sake, replace the batteries every month with the best quality batteries available.

and soothing words should help console him, as well as just putting him down and letting him explore on his own (under your watchful eye, of course).

The pup may approach the family members or may busy himself with exploring for awhile. Gradually, each person should spend some time with the pup, one at a time, crouching down to get as close to the pup's level as possible and letting him sniff their hands and petting him gently. He definitely needs human attention and he needs to be touched—this is how to form an immediate bond. Just remember that the pup is experiencing a lot of things for the first time, all at the same time. There are new people, new noises, new smells and new things to investigate; so be gentle, be affectionate and be as comforting as you can.

YOUR PUP'S FIRST NIGHT HOME

You have traveled home with your new charge safely in his crate or on a friendly lap. He's been to the vet for a thorough check-up; he's been weighed, his papers examined; perhaps he's even been vaccinated and wormed as well. He's met the family, licked the whole family, including the excited children and the less-than-happy cat. He's explored his area, his new bed, the yard and anywhere else he's been permitted. He's eaten his first meal at home and relieved himself in the proper place. He's heard lots of new sounds, smelled new friends and seen more of the outside world than ever before.

That was the just the first day! He's tuckered out and is ready for bed...or so you think!

It's puppy's first night and you are ready to say "Good night"—keep in mind that this is puppy's first night ever to be sleeping alone. His dam and littermates are no longer at paw's length and he's a bit scared, cold and lonely. Be reassuring to your new family member. This is not the time to spoil him and give in to his inevitable whining.

Puppies whine. They whine to let others know where they are and hopefully to get company out of it. Place your pup in his new bed or crate in his room and close the door. Mercifully, he will fall asleep without a peep. When the inevitable occurs, ignore the whining; he is fine. Be strong and keep his interest in mind. Do not allow your heart to become guilty and visit the pup. He will fall asleep.

Many breeders recommend placing a piece of bedding from his former home in his new bed so that he recognizes the scent of his littermates. Others still advise placing a hot water bottle in his bed for warmth. This latter may be a good idea provided the pup doesn't attempt to suckle— he'll get good and wet and may not fall asleep so fast.

Puppy's first night can be somewhat stressful for the pup and his new family. Remember that you are setting the tone of nighttime at your house. Unless you want to play with your pup every night at 10 p.m., midnight

TOXIC PLANTS

Many plants can be toxic to dogs. If you see your dog carrying a piece of vegetation in his mouth, approach him in a quiet, disinterested manner, avoid eye contact, pet him and gradually remove the plant from his mouth. Alternatively, offer him a treat and maybe he'll drop the plant on his own accord. Be sure no toxic plants are growing in your own yard or garden.

and 2 a.m., don't initiate the habit. Surely your family will thank you, and so will your pup!

PREVENTING PUPPY PROBLEMS

SOCIALIZATION

Now that you have done all of the preparatory work and have helped your pup get accustomed to his new home and family, it is about time for you to have some fun! Socializing your Siberian Husky pup gives you the opportunity to show off your new friend, and your pup gets to reap the benefits of being an adorable furry creature that people will coo over, want to pet and, in general, think is absolutely precious!

Besides getting to know his new family, your puppy should be exposed to other people, animals and situations. This will help him become well adjusted as he grows up and less prone to being timid or fearful of the new things he will encounter. Your pup's socialization began at the breeder's, now it is your responsibility to continue. The socialization he receives up until the age of 12 weeks is the most critical, as this is the time when he forms his impressions of the outside world. Lack of socialization can manifest itself in fear and aggression as the dog grows up. He needs lots of human contact, affection, handling and exposure to other animals. Be careful during the eight-to-ten-week-old period, also known as the fear period. The interaction he receives during this time should be gentle and reassuring.

Once your pup has received his necessary vaccinations, feel free to take him out and about (on his lead, of course). Take him around the neighborhood, take him on your daily errands, let people pet him, let him meet other dogs and pets, etc. Puppies do not have to try to make friends; there will be no shortage of people who will want to introduce themselves. Just make sure that you carefully supervise each meeting. If the neighborhood children want

---

SOCIALIZATION

Thorough socialization includes not only meeting new people but also being introduced to new experiences such as riding in the car, having his coat brushed, hearing the television, walking in a crowd—the list is endless. The more your pup experiences, and the more positive the experiences are, the less of a shock and the less frightening it will be for your pup to encounter new things.

to say hello, for example, that is great—children and Husky pups make great companions. But sometimes an excited child can unintentionally handle a pup too roughly, or an overzealous pup can playfully nip a little too hard. You want to make socialization experiences positive ones; what a pup learns during this very formative stage will impact his attitude toward future encounters. A pup that has a bad experience with a child may grow up to be a dog that is shy around or aggressive toward children, and you want your dog to be comfortable around everyone.

CHEWING TIPS

Chewing goes hand in hand with nipping in the sense that a teething puppy is always looking for a way to soothe his aching gums. In this case, instead of chewing on you, he may have taken a liking to your favorite shoe or something else which he should not be chewing. Again, realize that this is a normal canine behavior that does not need to be discouraged, only redirected. Your pup just needs to be taught what is acceptable to chew on and what is off-limits. Consistently tell him "No!" when you catch him chewing on something forbidden and give him a chew toy.

Conversely, praise him when you catch him chewing on something appropriate. In this way you are discouraging the inappropriate behavior and reinforcing the desired behavior. The puppy chewing should stop after his adult teeth have come in, but an adult dog continues to chew for various reasons—perhaps because he is bored, needs to relieve tension or just likes to chew. That is why it is important to redirect his chewing when he is still young.

Puppies must be socialized. They must get to know people, other dogs and other animals so they will not be afraid of them in the future. Most of all, puppies need love and affection.

CONSISTENCY IN TRAINING

Dogs, being pack animals, naturally need a leader, or else they try to establish dominance in their packs. When you bring a dog into your family, who becomes the leader and who

TRAINING TIP
Training your puppy takes much patience and can be frustrating at times, but you should see results from your efforts. If you have a puppy that seems untrainable, take him to a trainer or behaviorist. The dog may have a personality problem that requires the help of a professional, or perhaps you need help in learning how to train your dog.

and make sure that all family members do the same. It will only confuse the pup when Mother tells him to get off the couch when he is used to sitting up there with Father to watch the nightly news. Avoid discrepancies by having all members of the household decide on the rules before the pup even comes home...and be consistent in enforcing them! Early training shapes the dog's personality, so you cannot be unclear in what you expect.

becomes the "pack" are entirely up to you! Your pup's intuitive quest for dominance, coupled with the fact that it is nearly impossible to look at an adorable Siberian Husky pup with his ice-blue eyes and not cave in, give the pup almost an unfair advantage in getting the upper hand! And a pup will definitely

Dogs are pack animals and they need a leader. Every time two dogs meet, they size each other up to determine which of them is the leader and which is the follower.

test the waters to see what he can and cannot get away with. Do not give in to those pleading eyes—stand your ground when it comes to disciplining the pup

COMMON PUPPY PROBLEMS
The best way to prevent problems is to be proactive in stopping an undesirable behavior as soon as it starts. The old saying "You can't teach an old dog new tricks" does not necessarily hold true, but it is true that it is much easier to discourage bad behavior in a young developing pup than to wait until the pup's bad behavior becomes the adult dog's bad habit. There are some problems that are especially prevalent in puppies as they develop.

NIPPING
As puppies start to teethe, they feel the need to sink their teeth into anything...unfortunately that includes your fingers, arms, hair, toes...whatever happens to be available. You may find this

behavior cute for about the first five seconds...until you feel just how sharp those puppy teeth are. This is something you want to discourage immediately and consistently with a firm "No!" (or whatever number of firm "Nos" it takes for him to understand that you mean business) and replace your finger with an appropriate chew toy. While this behavior is merely annoying when the dog is still young, it can become dangerous as your Siberian Husky's adult teeth grow in and his jaws develop if he thinks that it is okay to gnaw on human appendages. Your Siberian Husky does not mean any harm with a friendly nip, but he also does not know that this is unacceptable behavior unless you teach him otherwise.

CRYING/WHINING
Your pup will often cry, whine, whimper, howl or make some type of commotion when he is left alone. This is basically his way of calling out for attention, of calling out to make sure that you know he is there and that you have not forgotten about him. He feels insecure when he is left alone, for example, when you are out of the house and he is in his crate or when you are in another part of the house and he cannot see you. The noise he is making is an expression of the anxiety he feels at being alone, so he needs to be taught that being alone is okay. You are not actually training the dog to stop making noise, you are training him to feel comfortable when he is alone and thus removing the need for him to make the noise. This is where the crate with a cozy blanket and a favorite toy comes in handy. You want to know that he is safe when you are not there to supervise and you know that he will be safe in his crate rather than roaming freely about the house. In order for the pup to stay in his crate without making a fuss, he needs to be comfortable in his crate. On that note, it is extremely important that the crate is never used as a form of punishment, or the pup will have a negative association with the crate.

Accustom the pup to the crate in short, gradually increasing time intervals in which you put him in the crate, maybe with a treat, and stay in the room with him. If he cries or makes a fuss, do not go to him, but stay in his sight. Gradually he will realize that staying in his crate is all right without your help, and it will not be so traumatic for him when you are not around. You may want to leave the radio on softly when you leave the house; the sound of human voices may be comforting to him.

DIETARY AND FEEDING CONSIDERATIONS

You have probably heard it a thousand times; you are what you eat. Believe it or not, it's very true. For dogs, they are what you feed them because they have little choice in the matter. Even those people who truly want to feed their dogs the best often cannot do so because they do not know which foods are best for their dogs.

Dog foods are produced in three basic types: dry, semi-moist and canned. Dry foods are for the cost-conscious because they are much less expensive than semi-moist and canned. Dry foods contain the least fat and the most preservatives. Most canned foods are 60–70 percent water, while semi-moist foods are so full of sugar that they are the least preferred by owners, though dogs welcome them (as does a child candy).

Three stages of development must be considered when selecting a diet for your dog: the puppy stage, the mid-age or adult stage and the senior stage.

PUPPY DIETS

Puppies have a natural instinct to suck milk from their mother's teats. They should exhibit this behavior the first day of their lives. If they don't suckle within a few hours, the breeder should attempt to put them onto their mother's nipples. Their failure to feed means that the breeder has to feed the pups himself under the advice and guidance of a veterinarian. This will involve a baby bottle and a special formula. Their mother's milk is much better than any formula because it contains colostrum, a sort of antibiotic milk that protects the puppy during the first eight to ten

CHANGE IN DIET

As your dog's caretaker, you know the importance of keeping his diet consistent, but sometimes when you run out of food or if you're on vacation, you have to make a change quickly. Some dogs will experience digestive problems, but most will not. If you are planning on changing your dog's menu, do so gradually to ensure that your dog will not have any problems. Over a period of four to five days, slowly add some new food to your dog's old food, increasing the percentage of new food each day.

The breeder will introduce the pups to solid food. New owners are advised to resume feeding the same brand and the same schedule as begun by the breeder.

weeks of their lives.

Puppies should be allowed to nurse for six weeks and they should be slowly weaned away from their mother by introducing small portions of canned meat after they are about one month old.

By the time they are eight weeks old, they should be completely weaned and fed solely a puppy dry food. Selection of a complete, quality puppy food is most important as the puppy grows fastest during its first year of life. Growth foods can be recommended by your veterinarian and the puppy should be kept on this diet for up to 18 months.

Puppy diets should be balanced for your dog's needs and supplements of vitamins, minerals and protein should not be necessary.

ADULT DIETS

A dog is considered an adult when it has stopped growing. The growth is in height and/or length. Do not consider the dog's

TEST FOR PROPER DIET

A good test for proper diet is the color, odor and firmness of your dog's stool. A healthy dog usually produces three semi-hard stools per day. The stools should have no unpleasant odor. They should be the same color from excretion to excretion.

A Siberian Husky reaches adulthood between two and three years of age, though some dogs fully mature between 16 and 24 months, while others may take the whole three years.

An interesting veterinary finding regarding the nutrition of Siberian Huskies, and other sled-type dogs, reports the positive effect of zinc supplementation on the breed. Certain skin disorders, specifically called zinc-responsive dermatosis, can be cleared by utilizing a zinc supplement. Depending on the dog food you choose for your Siberian Husky, certain foods can impair the body's utilization of zinc and therefore require supplementation. Seek the advice of your vet.

DIETS FOR SENIOR DOGS
As dogs get older, their metabolism changes. The older dog usually exercises less, moves more slowly and sleeps more. This change in lifestyle and physiological performance requires a change in diet. Since these changes take place slowly, they might not be recognizable. What is easily recognizable is weight gain. By continually feeding your dog an adult maintenance diet when it is slowing down metabolically, your dog will gain weight. Obesity in an older dog compounds the health problems

weight when the decision is made to switch from a puppy diet to a maintenance diet. Again you should rely upon your veterinarian to recommend an acceptable maintenance diet. Major dog-food manufacturers specialize in this type of food and it is just necessary for you to select the one best suited to your dog's needs. Active dogs may have different requirements than sedate dogs.

that already accompany old age.

As your dog gets older, few of their organs function up to par. The kidneys slow down and the intestines become less efficient. These age-related factors are best handled with a change in diet and a change in feeding schedule to give smaller portions that are more easily digested.

There is no single best diet for every older dog. While many dogs do well on light or senior diets, other dogs do better on puppy diets or other special premium diets such as lamb and rice. Be sensitive to your senior Siberian Husky's diet and this will help control other problems that may arise with your old friend.

GRAIN-BASED DIETS

Some less expensive dog foods are based on grains and other plant proteins. While these products may appear to be attractively priced, many breeders prefer a diet based on animal proteins and believe that they are more conducive to your dog's health. Many grain-based diets rely on soy protein, which may cause flatulence (passing gas).

There are many cases, however, when your dog might require a special diet. These special requirements should only be recommended by your veterinarian.

WATER

Just as your dog needs proper nutrition from his food, water is an essential "nutrient" as well. Water keeps the dog's body properly hydrated and promotes normal function of the body's systems. During housebreaking it is necessary to keep an eye on how much water your Siberian Husky is drinking, but once he is reliably trained he should have access to clean fresh water at all times. Make sure that the dog's water bowl is clean, and change the water often.

Adult dogs may eat once or twice a day. Select a premium brand to keep your Husky in top condition.

Your local pet shop usually carries a complete range of grooming tools to help you maintain your Husky's woolly coat.

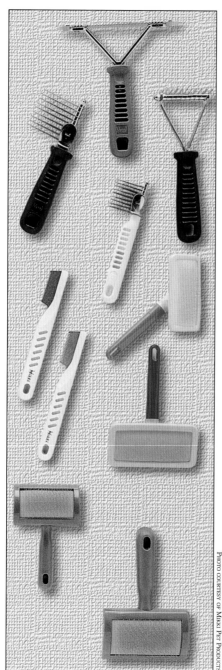

PHOTO COURTESY OF MIKKI PET PRODUCTS.

EXERCISE

All dogs require some form of exercise, regardless of breed. A sedentary lifestyle is as harmful to a dog as it is to a person. The Siberian Husky happens to be an active breed that requires more exercise than, say, an English Bulldog, but you don't have to be a weightlifter or marathon runner to provide your dog with the exercise he needs. Regular walks, play sessions in the yard or letting the dog run free in the yard under your supervision are all sufficient forms of exercise for the Siberian Husky. For those who are more ambitious, you will find that your Siberian Husky will be able to keep up with you on extra-long walks or the morning run. Not only is exercise essential to keep the dog's body fit, it is essential to his mental well-being. A bored dog will find something to do, which often manifests itself in some type of destructive behavior. In this sense, it is essential for the owner's mental well-being as well!

GROOMING YOUR HUSKY

GROOMING CONSIDERATIONS
To look at the Siberian Husky's beautiful, thick coat, one might think that much grooming and special attention is required. While regular maintenance is

A Worthy Investment

Veterinary studies have proven that a
balanced high-quality diet pays off in your
dog's coat quality, behavior and activity
level. Invest in premium brands for the
maximum payoff with your dog.

Your Siberian puppy should be brushed daily. Your puppy should enjoy the brushing if you start when he is young.

(FACING PAGE) The normal, healthy hairs of a typical dog enlarged about 200 times natural size. The inset shows the tip of a fine, growing hair about 2,000 times natural size.

necessary, *natural* is the key to the Husky's beauty. From pet dog to Best in Show champion, the Husky's coat should be kept in its natural state without fancy clipping and elaborate grooming. The Husky's coat doesn't need it! The main goal in grooming the Siberian Husky is to keep the dog's coat looking good and in healthy condition. Siberian Huskies do shed, so during shedding seasons you will need to pay more attention to his coat. A metal rake or comb will aid in removing mats from the undercoat. A vigorous brushing will loosen much of the dead hair. Follow up with a metal comb to remove the hair that is being shed.

BRUSHING
A natural bristle brush or a slicker brush can be used for regular routine brushing. Daily brushing is effective for removing dead hair and stimulating the dog's natural oils to add shine and a healthy look to the coat. Your Siberian

Husky, prized for his natural appearance, is not a breed that needs excessive grooming, but his heavy coat needs to be brushed daily as part of routine maintenance. Daily brushing will minimize tangles and mats, get rid of dust and dandruff and remove any dead hair. Regular grooming sessions are also a good way to spend time with your dog. Many dogs grow to like the feel of being brushed and will enjoy the daily routine.

BATHING
Dogs do not need to be bathed as often as humans, but regular bathing is essential for healthy skin and shiny coat. Again, like most anything, if you accustom

GROOMING EQUIPMENT
How much grooming equipment you purchase will depend on how much grooming you are going to do. Here are some basics:
- Natural bristle brush
- Slicker brush
- Metal comb
- Metal rake
- Scissors
- Blow dryer
- Rubber mat
- Dog shampoo
- Spray hose attachment
- Ear cleaner
- Cotton balls
- Towels
- Nail clippers

Huskies are easily motivated by food. Food should only be used to introduce a new exercise. If you overdo it, your Husky will think of his lessons as an extra meal!

If you are dealing with a dog who insists on pulling you around, simply "put on your brakes" and stand your ground until the dog realizes that the two of you are not going anywhere until he is beside you and moving at your pace, not his. It may take some time just standing there to convince the dog that you are the leader and you will be the one to decide on the direction and speed of your travel.

Each time the dog looks up at you or slows down to give a slack lead between the two of you, quietly praise him and say, "Good heel. Good dog." Eventually, the dog will begin to respond and within a few days he will be walking politely beside you without pulling on the lead. At first, the training sessions should be kept short and very positive; soon the dog will be able to walk nicely with you for increasingly longer distances. Remember also

to give the dog free time and the opportunity to run and play when you are done with heel practice.

WEANING OFF FOOD IN TRAINING

Food is used in training new behaviors, yet once the dog understands what behavior goes with a specific command, it is time to start weaning him off the food treats. At first, give a treat after each exercise. Then, start to give a treat only after every other exercise. Mix up the times when you offer a food reward and the times when you only offer praise so that the dog will never know when he is going to receive both food and praise and when he is going to receive only praise. This is called a variable-ratio reward system and it proves successful because there is always the chance that the owner will produce a treat, so the dog

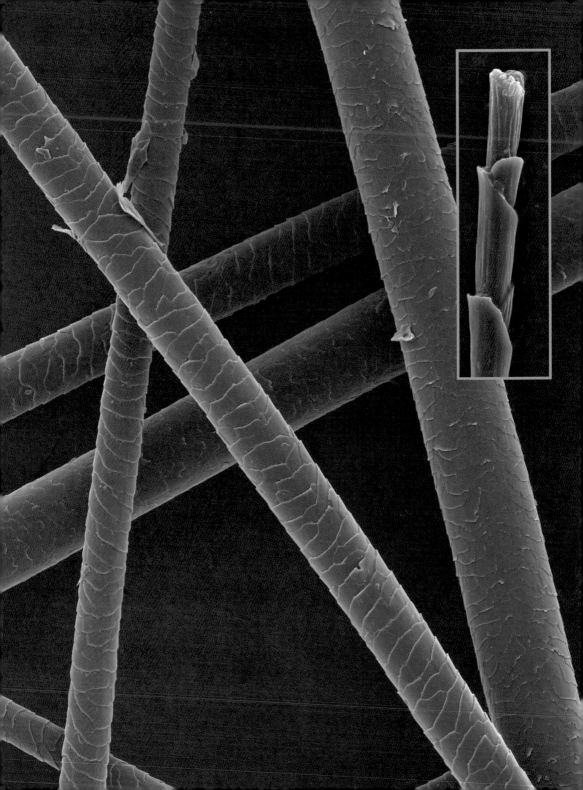

Your puppy should be accustomed to having his feet handled so that you can clip his nails and keep the excess hair on his feet trimmed.

your pup to being bathed as a puppy, it will be second nature by the time he grows up. You want your dog to be at ease in the bath or else it could end up a wet, soapy, messy ordeal for both of you!

Brush your Siberian Husky thoroughly before wetting his coat. This will get rid of most mats and tangles, which are harder to remove when the coat is wet. Make sure that your dog has a good non-slip surface to stand on. Begin by wetting the dog's coat. A shower or hose attachment is necessary for thoroughly wetting and rinsing the coat. Check the water temperature to make sure that it is neither too hot nor too cold.

Next, apply shampoo to the dog's coat and work it into a good lather. You should purchase a shampoo that is made for dogs; do not use a product made for human hair. Wash the head last; you do not want shampoo to drip into the dog's eyes while you are washing the rest of him. Work the shampoo all the way down to the skin. You can use this opportunity to check the skin for bumps, bites or other abnormalities. Do not neglect any area of the body—get all of the hard-to-reach places.

BATHING BEAUTY

Once you are sure that the dog is thoroughly rinsed, squeeze the excess water out of his coat with your hand and dry him with a heavy towel. You may choose to use a blow dryer on his coat or just let it dry naturally. In cold weather, never allow your dog outside with a wet coat.

There are "dry bath" products on the market, which are sprays and powders intended for spot cleaning, that can be used between regular baths if necessary. They are not substitutes for regular baths, but they are easy to use for touch-ups as they do not require rinsing.

EAR CLEANING

The ears should be kept clean and any excess hair inside the ear should be trimmed. Ears can be cleaned with a cotton ball and special cleaner or ear powder made especially for dogs. Be on the lookout for any signs of infection or ear-mite infestation. If your Siberian Husky has been shaking his head or scratching at his ears frequently, this usually indicates a problem. If his ears have an unusual odor, this is a sure sign of mite infestation or infection, and a signal to have his ears checked by the veterinarian.

NAIL CLIPPING

Your Siberian Husky should be accustomed to having his nails trimmed at an early age, since it

The nails must not be cut shorter than the quick. The quick is easy to see in light-colored nails, but hard to see in dark nails. When clipping your Husky's nails, cut only a little at a time to minimize the risk of cutting the quick.

Once the dog has been thoroughly shampooed, he requires an equally thorough rinsing. Shampoo left in the coat can be irritating to the skin. Protect his eyes from the shampoo by shielding them with your hand and directing the flow of water in the opposite direction. You should also avoid getting water in the ear canal. Be prepared for your dog to shake out his coat—you might want to stand back, but make sure you have a hold on the dog to keep him from running through the house.

PEDICURE TIP

A dog that spends a lot of time outside on a hard surface, such as cement or pavement, will have his nails naturally worn down and may not need to have them trimmed as often, except maybe during times when he is not outside as much. Regardless, it is best to get your dog accustomed to the nail-trimming procedure at an early age so that he is used to it. Some dogs are especially sensitive about having their feet touched, but if a dog has experienced it since puppyhood, it should not bother him.

will be part of your maintenance routine throughout his life. Not only does it look nicer, but a dog with long nails can cause injury if he jumps up or if he scratches someone unintentionally. Also, a long nail has a better chance of ripping and bleeding, or causing the feet to spread. A good rule of thumb is that if you can hear your dog's nails' clicking on the floor when he walks, his nails are too long.

Before you start cutting, make sure you can identify the "quick" in each nail. The quick is a blood vessel that runs through the center of each nail and grows rather close to the end. It will bleed if accidentally cut, which will be quite painful for the dog as it contains nerve endings. Keep some type of clotting agent on hand, such as a styptic pencil or styptic powder (the type used for shaving). This will stop the bleeding quickly when applied to the end of the cut nail. Do not panic if this happens, just stop the bleeding

> ## ON THE ROAD
> If you are going on a long road trip with your dog, be sure the hotels are dog-friendly. Many hotels do not accept dogs or may have restrictions about guests and their dogs. Also take along some ice that can be thawed and offered to your dog if he becomes overheated. Most dogs like to lick ice.

and talk soothingly to your dog. Once he has calmed down, move on to the next nail. It is better to clip a little at a time, particularly with black-nailed dogs.

Hold your pup steady as you begin trimming his nails; you do not want him to make any sudden movements or run away. Talk to him soothingly and stroke his fur as you clip. Holding his foot in your hand, simply take off the end of each nail in one quick clip. You can purchase nail clippers that are specially made for dogs; you can probably find them wherever you buy pet or grooming supplies.

TRAVELING WITH YOUR DOG

CAR TRAVEL
You should accustom your Siberian Husky to riding in a car at an early age. You may or may not often take him in the car, but at the very least he will

Never take any dog into your car unless he is crated. This ensures safety for both you and the dog.

need to go to the vet and you do not want these trips to be traumatic for the dog or a big hassle for you. The safest way for a dog to ride in the car is in his crate. If he uses a fiberglass crate in the house, you can use the same crate for travel. If you have a wire crate in the house, consider purchasing an appropriately sized fiberglass or wooden crate for traveling. Wire crates can be used for travel, but fiberglass or wooden crates are safer.

Put the pup in the crate and see how he reacts. If he seems uneasy, you can have a passenger hold him on his lap while you drive. Another option is a specially made safety harness for dogs, which straps the dog in much like a seat belt. Do not let the dog roam loose in the vehicle—this is very dangerous! If you should stop short, your dog can be thrown and injured. If the dog starts climbing on you and pestering you while you are driving, you will not be able to concentrate on the road. It is an unsafe situation for everyone—human and canine.

For long trips, be prepared to stop to let the dog relieve himself. Bring along whatever you need to clean up after him. You also should bring along some paper towels and rags, should he have an accident in the car or become carsick.

AIR TRAVEL

If bringing your dog on a flight, you will have to contact the airline to make special arrangements. Each airline has different requirements, so be sure to contact the airline well in advance. The dog will be required to travel in a fiberglass crate; you may be able to use your own or the airline can usually supply one. To help the dog be at ease, put one of his favorite toys in the crate with him. Do not feed the dog for several hours before checking in to minimize his need to relieve himself. However, certain regulations specify that you must attach a water bowl and possibly some food to the dog's crate.

Make sure your dog is properly identified and that your contact information appears on his ID tags and on his crate. Animals travel in a different area of the plane than human

TOO HOT TO HANDLE

Never leave your dog alone in the car. In hot weather, your dog can die from the high temperature inside a closed vehicle; even a car parked in the shade can heat up very quickly. Leaving the window open is dangerous as well since the dog can hurt himself trying to get out.

passengers, and, although transporting animals is routine for large airlines, there is always that slight risk of getting separated from your dog.

BOARDING & VACATIONS
So you want to take a family vacation—and you want to include *all* members of the family. You would probably

Every dog must have its identification tags attached to its collar at all times.

make arrangements for accommodations ahead of time anyway, but this is especially important when traveling with a dog. You do not want to make an overnight stop at the only place around for miles to find out that they do not allow dogs. Also, you do not want to reserve a place for your family without mentioning that you are bringing a dog, because if it is against their policy, you may not have a place to stay.

Alternatively, if you are traveling and choose not to bring your Siberian Husky, you will have to make arrangements for him while you are away. Some options are to bring him to a neighbor's house to stay while you are gone, to have a trusted neighbor stop by often or stay at your house or to bring your dog to a reputable boarding kennel. If you choose to board him at a kennel, you should stop by to see the facility and where the dogs are kept to make sure that it is clean. Talk to some of the employees and see how they treat the dogs—do they spend time with the dogs, play with them, exercise them, etc.? You know that your Siberian Husky will not be happy unless he gets regular activity. Also find out the kennel's policy on vaccinations and what they require. This is for all of the dogs' safety, since when dogs are kept together, there is a greater risk of diseases being passed from dog to dog. Many veterinarians offer boarding facilities; this is another option.

LOST AND FOUND
You have a valuable dog. If the dog is lost or stolen, you would undoubtedly become extremely upset. Likewise, if you encounter a lost dog, notify the police or the local animal shelter.

IDENTIFICATION OPTIONS

As puppies become more and more expensive, especially those puppies of high quality for showing and/or breeding, they have a greater chance of being stolen. The usual collar dog tag is, of course, easily removed. But there are two more permanent techniques that have become widely used for identification.

The puppy microchip implantation involves the injection of a small microchip, about the size of a corn kernel, under the skin of the dog. If your dog shows up at a clinic or shelter, or is offered for resale under less-than-savory circumstances, it can be positively identified by the microchip. The microchip is scanned, and a registry quickly identifies you as the owner.

Tattooing is done on various parts of the dog, from his belly to his cheeks. The number tattooed can be your telephone number or any other number that you can easily memorize. When professional dog thieves see a tattooed dog, they usually lose interest. Both microchipping and tattooing can be done at your local veterinary clinic. For the safety of our dogs, no laboratory facility or dog broker will accept a tattooed dog as stock.

Discuss microchipping and tattooing with your vet and breeder. Vets and some breeders perform these services on their own premises for a reasonable fee. Be certain that the dog is then properly registered with a national database.

IDENTIFICATION

Your dog is your valued companion and friend. That is why you always keep a close eye on him and you have made sure that he cannot escape from the yard or wriggle out of his collar and run away from you. However, accidents can happen and there may come a time when your dog unexpectedly gets separated from you. If this unfortunate event should occur, the first thing on your mind will be finding him. Proper identification will increase the chances of his being returned to you safely.

Your Husky puppy relies on you for his safety. Be wise and take precautions.

Living with an untrained dog is a lot like owning a piano that you do not know how to play—it is a nice object to look at but it does not do much more than that to bring you pleasure. Now try taking piano lessons and suddenly the piano comes alive and brings forth magical sounds and rhythms that set your heart singing and your body swaying.

The same is true with your Siberian Husky. At first you enjoy seeing him around the house. He does not do much with you other than need food, water and

The young Siberian Husky puppy is a dry sponge ready to soak up whatever you teach him. Take advantage of your new puppy's willingness to learn and to pay attention for his lessons.

exercise. Come to think of it, he does not bring you much joy, either. He is a big responsibility with a very small return. And often, he develops unacceptable behaviors that annoy and/or infuriate you, to say nothing of bad habits that may end up costing you great sums of money. Not a good thing!

Now train your Siberian Husky. Enroll in an obedience class. Teach him good manners as you learn how and why he behaves the way he does. Find out how to communicate with your dog and how to recognize and understand his communications with you. Suddenly the dog takes on a new role in your life—he is smart, interesting, well behaved and fun to be with, and he demonstrates his bond of devotion to you daily. In other words, your Siberian Husky does wonders for your ego because he constantly reminds you that you are not only his leader, you are his hero! Miraculous things have happened—you have a wonderful dog (even your family and friends have noticed the transformation!) and you feel good about yourself.

Those involved with teaching dog obedience and counseling

owners about their dogs' behavior have discovered some interesting facts about dog ownership. For example, training dogs when they are puppies results in the highest rate of success in developing well-mannered and well-adjusted adult dogs. Training an older dog, say from six months to six years of age, can produce almost equal results providing that the owner accepts the dog's slower rate of learning capability and is willing to work patiently to help the dog succeed at developing to his fullest potential. Unfortunately, the patience factor is what many owners of untrained adult dogs lack, so they do not persist until their dogs are successful at learning particular behaviors.

Training a puppy, for example, aged 8 to 16 weeks (20 weeks at the most) is like working with a dry sponge in a pool of water. The pup soaks up whatever you show him and constantly looks for more things to do and learn. At this early age, his body is not yet producing hormones, and therein lies the reason for such a high rate of success. Without hormones, he is focused on his owners and not particularly interested in investigating other places, dogs, people, etc. You are his leader; his provider of food, water, shelter and security. Therefore, he latches onto you and wants to stay close. He will usually follow you from room to room, will not let you out of his sight when you are outdoors with him, and will respond in like manner to the people and animals you encounter. If, for example, you greet a friend warmly, he will be happy to greet the person as well. If, however, you are hesitant or anxious about the approach of a stranger, he will respond accordingly.

Once the puppy begins to produce hormones, his natural curiosity emerges and he begins to investigate the world around him. It is at that time when you may notice that the untrained dog begins to wander away from you and even ignore your commands to stay close. When this behavior becomes a problem, the owner has two choices: get rid of the dog or train him. It is strongly urged that you choose the latter option.

Occasionally there are no classes available within a reasonable distance from the owner's home. Sometimes there are classes available but the tuition is too costly. Whatever the circumstances, the solution to training your dog without obedience classes lies within the pages of this book. This chapter is devoted to helping you train your Siberian Husky at home. If the recommended procedures are followed faithfully, you may expect positive results that will prove rewarding to both you and your dog.

Whether your Siberian Husky is a puppy or a mature adult, the methods of teaching and the techniques we use in training basic behaviors are the same. After all, every dog, whether puppy or adult, responds favorably to gentle motivational methods and sincere praise and encouragement. Now let us get started.

HOUSEBREAKING

You can train a puppy to relieve itself wherever you choose. For example, city dwellers often train their puppies to relieve themselves in the gutter because large plots of grass are not readily available. Suburbanites, on the other hand, usually have yards to accommodate their dogs' needs.

Outdoor training includes such surfaces as grass, dirt and cement. Indoor training usually means training your dog to newspaper.

When deciding on the surface and location that you will want your Siberian Husky to use, be sure it is going to be permanent. Training your dog to grass and then changing your mind two months later is extremely difficult for both dog and owner.

Next, choose the command you will use each and every time you want your puppy to void. "Go hurry up" and "Let's go" are examples of commands commonly used by dog owners.

> ### HOUSE-TRAINING TIP
> Most of all, be consistent. Always take your dog to the same location, always use the same command and always have the dog on lead when he is in his relief area, unless a fenced-in yard is available.
>
> By following the Success Method, your puppy will be completely housebroken by the time his muscle and brain development reach maturity. Keep in mind that small breeds usually mature faster than large breeds, but all puppies should be trained by six months of age.

Get in the habit of asking the puppy, "Do you want to go hurry up?" (or whatever your chosen relief command is) before you take him out. That way, when he becomes an adult, you will be able to determine if he wants to go out when you ask him. A confirmation will be signs of interest, such as wagging his tail, watching you intently, going to the door, etc.

PUPPY'S NEEDS

The puppy needs to relieve himself after play periods, after each meal, after he has been sleeping and any time he indicates that he is looking for a place to relieve himself.

The urinary and intestinal tract muscles of very young puppies are not fully developed.

Canine Development Schedule

It is important to understand how and at what age a puppy develops into adulthood. If you are a puppy owner, consult the following Canine Development Schedule to determine the stage of development your Siberian Husky puppy is currently experiencing. This knowledge will help you as you work with the puppy in the weeks and months ahead.

Period	Age	Characteristics
FIRST TO THIRD	BIRTH TO SEVEN WEEKS	Puppy needs food, sleep and warmth, and responds to simple and gentle touching. Needs mother for security and disciplining. Needs littermates for learning and interacting with other dogs. Pup learns to function within a pack and learns pack order of dominance. Begin socializing with adults and children for short periods. Begins to become aware of its environment.
FOURTH	EIGHT TO TWELVE WEEKS	Brain is fully developed. Needs socializing with outside world. Remove from mother and littermates. Needs to change from canine pack to human pack. Human dominance necessary. Fear period occurs between 8 and 16 weeks. Avoid fright and pain.
FIFTH	THIRTEEN TO SIXTEEN WEEKS	Training and formal obedience should begin. Less association with other dogs, more with people, places, situations. Period will pass easily if you remember this is pup's change-to-adolescence time. Be firm and fair. Flight instinct prominent. Permissiveness and over-disciplining can do permanent damage. Praise for good behavior.
JUVENILE	FOUR TO EIGHT MONTHS	Another fear period about 7 to 8 months of age. It passes quickly, but be cautious of fright and pain. Sexual maturity reached. Dominant traits established. Dog should understand sit, down, come and stay by now.

NOTE: THESE ARE APPROXIMATE TIME FRAMES. ALLOW FOR INDIVIDUAL DIFFERENCES IN PUPPIES.

THE SUCCESS METHOD

Success that comes by luck is usually short-lived. Success that comes by well-thought-out proven methods is often more easily achieved and permanent. This is the Success Method. It is designed to give you, the puppy owner, a simple yet proven way to help your puppy develop clean living habits and a feeling of security in his new environment. Follow the steps outlined here for success!

Therefore, like human babies, puppies need to relieve themselves frequently.

Take your puppy out often—every hour for an eight-week-old, for example. The older the puppy, the less often he will need to relieve himself. Finally, as a mature healthy adult, he will require only three to five relief trips per day.

HOUSING

Huskies trained to relieve themselves on grass will always seek out this surface to do so.

Since the types of housing and control you provide for your puppy have a direct relationship on the success of house-training, we consider the various aspects of both before we begin training.

Bringing a new puppy home and turning him loose in your house can be compared to turning a child loose in a sports arena and telling the child that the place is all his! The sheer enormity of the place would be too much for him to handle.

Instead, offer the puppy clearly defined areas where he can play, sleep, eat and live. A room of the house where the family gathers is the most obvious choice. Puppies are social animals and need to feel a part of the pack right from the start. Hearing your voice, watching you while you are doing things and smelling you nearby are all positive reinforcers that he is now a member of your pack. Usually a family room, the kitchen or a nearby adjoining breakfast nook is ideal for providing safety and security for both puppy and owner.

Within that room there should be a smaller area which the puppy can call his own. A cubbyhole, a wire or fiberglass

THE SUCCESS METHOD
6 Steps to Successful Crate Training

1 Tell the puppy "Crate time!" and place him in the crate with a small treat (a piece of cheese or half of a biscuit). Let him stay in the crate for five minutes while you are in the same room. Then release him and praise lavishly. Never release him when he is fussing. Wait until he is quiet before you let him out.

2 Repeat Step 1 several times a day.

3 The next day, place the puppy in the crate as before. Let him stay there for ten minutes. Do this several times.

4 Continue building time in five-minute increments until the puppy stays in his crate for 30 minutes with you in the room. Always take him to his relief area after prolonged periods in his crate.

5 Now go back to Step 1 and let the puppy stay in his crate for five minutes, this time while you are out of the room.

6 Once again, build crate time in five-minute increments with you out of the room. When the puppy will stay willingly in his crate (he may even fall asleep!) for 30 minutes with you out of the room, he will be ready to stay in it for several hours at a time.

dog crate or a fenced (not boarded!) corner from which he can view the activities of his new family will be fine. The size of the area or crate is the key factor here. The area must be large enough for the puppy to lie down and stretch out as well as stand up without rubbing his head on the top, yet small enough so that he cannot relieve himself at one end and sleep at the other without coming into contact with his droppings.

Dogs are, by nature, clean animals and will not remain close to their relief areas unless forced to do so. In those cases,

PRACTICE MAKES PERFECT!

- Have training lessons with your dog every day in several short segments—three to five times a day for a few minutes at a time is ideal.
- Do not have long practice sessions. The dog will become easily bored.
- Never practice when you are tired, ill, worried or in an otherwise negative mood. This will transmit to the dog and may have an adverse effect on its performance.

Think fun, short and above all positive! End each session on a high note, rather than a failed exercise, and make sure to give a lot of praise. Enjoy the training and help your dog enjoy it, too.

they then become dirty dogs and usually remain that way for life.

The crate or cubby should be lined with a nice crate pad or a clean towel and offer one toy, no more. Do not put food or water in the crate, as eating and drinking will activate his digestive processes and ultimately defeat your purpose as well as make the puppy very uncomfortable as he attempts to "hold it."

CONTROL

By control, we mean helping the puppy to create a lifestyle pattern that will be compatible to that of his human pack (*you!*). Just as we guide little children to learn our way of life, we must show the puppy when it is time to play, eat, sleep, exercise and even entertain himself.

Your puppy should always sleep in his crate. He should also learn that, during times of household confusion and excessive human activity such as at breakfast when family members are preparing for the day, he can play by himself in relative safety and comfort in his crate. Each time you leave the puppy alone, he should be crated. Puppies are chewers. They cannot tell the difference between lamp cords, television wires, shoes, table legs, etc. Chewing into a television wire, for example, can be fatal to the puppy, while a shorted wire can

start a fire in the house.

If the puppy chews on the arm of the chair when he is alone, you will probably discipline him angrily when you get home. Thus, he makes the association that your coming home means he is going to be punished. (He will not remember chewing the chair and is incapable of making the association of the discipline with his naughty deed.) Crating the pup prevents this from happening when you are out.

Other times of excitement, such as family parties, etc., can be fun for the puppy, providing he can view the activities from the security of his crate. He is not underfoot and he is not being fed all sorts of tidbits that will probably cause him stomach distress, yet he still feels a part of the fun.

SCHEDULE

As stated earlier, a puppy should be taken to his relief area each time he is released from his crate,

---

TAKE THE LEAD

Do not carry your dog to his relief area. Lead him there on a leash or, better yet, encourage him to follow you to the spot. If you start carrying him to his spot, you might end up doing this routine forever and your dog will have the satisfaction of having trained *you.*

after meals, after a play session, when he first awakens in the morning (at age 8 weeks, this can mean 5 a.m.!) and whenever he indicates by circling or sniffing busily that he needs to urinate or defecate. For a puppy less than ten weeks of age, a routine of taking him out every hour is necessary. As the puppy grows, he will be able to wait for longer periods of time.

Keep trips to his relief area short. Stay no more than five or six minutes and then return to the house. If he goes during that time, praise him lavishly and take him indoors immediately. If he does not, but he has an accident when you go back indoors, pick him up immediately, say "No! No!" and return to his relief area. Wait a few minutes, then return to the house again. Never hit a puppy or put his face in urine or excrement when he has an accident!

Once indoors, put the puppy in his crate until you have had time to clean up his accident. Then release him to the family area and watch him more closely than before. Chances are, his accident was a result of your not picking up his signal or waiting too long before offering him the opportunity to relieve himself. Never hold a grudge against the puppy for accidents.

Let the puppy learn that going outdoors means it is time to relieve himself, not play. Once

trained, he will be able to play indoors and out and still differentiate between the times for play versus the times for relief.

Help him develop regular hours for naps, being alone, playing by himself and just resting, all in his crate. Encourage him to entertain himself while you are busy with your activities. Let him learn that having you near is comforting, but it is not your main purpose in life to provide him with undivided attention.

Each time you put the puppy in his crate tell him, "Crate time!" (or whatever command you choose). Soon, he will run to his crate when he hears those words.

In the beginning of his training, do not leave him in his crate for prolonged periods of time except during the night when everyone is sleeping. Make his experience with his crate a pleasant one and, as an adult, he will love his crate and willingly stay in it for several hours. There are many people who go to work and leave their adult dogs crated while they are away. The dogs accept this as their lifestyle and look forward to "crate time."

Crate training provides safety for you, the puppy and the home. It also provides the puppy with a feeling of security, and that helps the puppy achieve self-confidence and clean habits.

Remember that one of the primary ingredients in house-training your puppy is control. Regardless of your lifestyle, there will always be occasions when you will need to have a place where your dog can stay and be happy and safe. Crate training is the answer for now and in the future.

In conclusion, a few key elements are really all you need for a successful house-training method—consistency, frequency, praise, control and supervision. By following these procedures with a normal, healthy puppy, you and the puppy will soon be past the stage of "accidents" and ready to move on to a full and rewarding life together.

ROLES OF DISCIPLINE, REWARD AND PUNISHMENT

Discipline, training one to act in accordance with rules, brings order to life. It is as simple as that. Without discipline, particularly in a group society, chaos

reigns supreme and the group will eventually perish. Humans and canines are social animals and need some form of discipline in order to function effectively. They must procure food, protect their home and their young and reproduce.

If there were no discipline in the lives of social animals, they would eventually die from starvation and/or predation by other stronger animals.

In the case of domestic canines, dogs need discipline in

> **ATTENTION!**
> Your dog is actually training you at the same time you are training him. Dogs do things to get attention. They usually repeat whatever succeeds in getting your attention.

their lives in order to understand how their pack (you and other family members) functions and how they must act in order to survive.

A large humane society in a highly populated area recently surveyed dog owners regarding their satisfaction with their relationships with their dogs. People who had trained their dogs were 75% more satisfied with their pets than those who had never trained their dogs.

Dr. Edward Thorndike, a

psychologist, established
Thorndike's Theory of Learning,
which states that a behavior that
results in a pleasant event tends
to be repeated. A behavior that
results in an unpleasant event
tends not to be repeated. It is this
theory on which training
methods are based today. For
example, if you manipulate a dog
to perform a specific behavior
and reward him for doing it, he
is likely to do it again because he
enjoyed the end result.

Occasionally, punishment, a
penalty inflicted for an offense, is
necessary. The best type of
punishment often comes from an
outside source. For example, a
child is told not to touch the
stove because he may get burned.
He disobeys and touches the
stove. In doing so, he receives a
burn. From that time on, he
respects the heat of the stove and
avoids contact with it. Therefore,
a behavior that results in an
unpleasant event tends not to be
repeated.

A good example of a dog's
learning the hard way is the dog
who chases the house cat. He is
told many times to leave the cat
alone, yet he persists in teasing
the cat. Then, one day, he begins
chasing the cat but the cat turns
and swipes a claw across the
dog's face, leaving him with a
painful gash on his nose. The
final result is that the dog stops
chasing the cat.

The buckle collar is the standard collar used for everyday purposes. Be sure that you adjust the buckle on growing puppies. Check it every day. It can become too tight overnight! These collars can be made of leather or nylon. Attach your dog's identification tags to this collar.

The choke chain is made for training. It is constructed of highly polished steel so that it slides easily through the stainless steel loop. The idea is that the dog controls the pressure around its neck and he will stop pulling if the collar becomes uncomfortable. *Never* leave a choke collar on your dog when not training.

The halter is for a trained dog that has to be restrained to prevent running away, chasing a cat and the like. Considered the most humane of all devices, it is frequently used on smaller dogs on which collars are not comfortable.

TRAINING EQUIPMENT

COLLAR

A simple buckle collar is fine for most dogs. One who pulls mightily on the leash may require a chain choker collar for training only. Most Huskies

Your Husky will be curious...especially where food is concerned! Any tendency toward begging and food stealing must be immediately discouraged.

respond quite naturally to the collar and rarely will the breed require a choke collar.

LEAD

A 3- to 6-foot lead is recommended, preferably made of leather, nylon or heavy cloth. A chain lead is not recommended, as many dog owners find that the chain cuts into their hands and that switching the lead back and forth frequently between their hands is painful.

TREATS

Have a bag of treats on hand. Something nutritious and easy to swallow works best; use a soft treat, a chunk of cheese or a piece of cooked chicken rather than a dry biscuit. By the time the dog gets done chewing a dry treat, he will forget why he is being rewarded in the first place! Using food rewards will not teach a dog to beg at the table—the only way to teach a dog to beg at the table is to give him food from the table. In training, rewarding the dog with a food treat away from the table will help him associate praise and the treats with learning new behaviors that obviously please his owner.

TRAINING BEGINS: ASK THE DOG A QUESTION

In order to teach your dog anything, you must first get his attention. After all, he cannot learn anything if he is looking away from you with his mind on something else.

To get his attention, ask him "School?" and immediately walk over to him and give him a treat as you tell him "Good

THINK BEFORE YOU BARK

Dogs are sensitive to their masters' moods and emotions. Use your voice wisely when communicating with your dog. Never raise your voice at your dog unless you are trying to correct him. "Barking" at your dog can become as meaningless as "dogspeak" is to you.

dog." Wait a minute or two and repeat the routine, this time with a treat in your hand as you approach the dog to within a foot of him. Do not go directly to him, but stop about a foot short of him and hold out the treat as you ask "School?" He will see you approaching with a treat in your hand and most likely begin walking toward you. As you meet, give him the treat and praise again.

The third time, ask the question, have a treat in your hand and walk only a short distance toward the dog so that he must walk almost all the way to you. As he reaches you, give him the treat and praise again.

By this time, the dog will probably be getting the idea that if he pays attention to you, especially when you ask that question, it will pay off in treats and fun activities for him. In other words, he learns that "school" means doing fun things with you that result in treats and positive attention for him.

Remember that the dog does not understand your verbal language, he only recognizes sounds. Your question translates to a series of sounds for him, and those sounds become the signal to go to you and pay attention; if he does, he will get to interact with you plus receive treats and praise.

THE GOLDEN RULE

The golden rule of dog training is simple. For each "question" (command), there is only one correct answer (reaction). One command = one reaction. Keep practicing the command until the dog reacts correctly without hesitating. Be repetitive but not monotonous. Dogs get bored just as people do!

THE BASIC COMMANDS

TEACHING SIT

Now that you have the dog's attention, hold the lead in your left hand and the food treat in your right. Place your food hand at the dog's nose and let him lick the treat but not take it from you. Say "Sit" and slowly raise your food hand from in front of the dog's nose up over his head so that he is looking at the ceiling.

Do not get frustrated while training your pup. With consistency and patience, you will have a well-behaved Husky before you know it.

As he bends his head upward, he will have to bend his knees to maintain his balance. As he bends his knees, he will assume a sit position. At that point, release the food treat and praise lavishly with comments such as "Good dog! Good sit!," etc. Remember to always praise enthusiastically, because dogs relish verbal praise from their owners and feel so proud of themselves whenever they accomplish a behavior.

You will not use food forever in getting the dog to obey your commands. Food is only used to teach new behaviors, and once the dog knows what you want when you give a specific command, you will wean him off of the food treats but still maintain the verbal praise. After all, you will always have your voice with you, but there will be many times when you have no food rewards yet you expect the dog to obey.

TEACHING DOWN

Teaching the down exercise is easy when you understand how the dog perceives the down position, and it is very difficult when you do not. In addition, teaching the down exercise using the wrong method can sometimes make the dog develop such a fear of the down that he either runs away when you say "down" or he attempts to bite the person who tries to force him down.

Have the dog sit close alongside your left leg, facing in the same direction as you are. Hold the lead in your left hand and a food treat in your right. Now place your left hand lightly on the top of the dog's shoulders where they meet above the spinal cord. Do not push down on the dog's shoulders; simply rest your left hand there so you can guide the dog to lie down close to your left leg rather than to swing away from your side when he drops.

Now place the food hand at the dog's nose, say "Down" very softly (almost a whisper) and slowly lower the food hand to the dog's front feet. When the food hand reaches the floor, begin moving it forward along the floor in front of the dog. Keep talking softly to the dog, saying things

---

LANGUAGE BARRIER

Dogs do not understand our language and have to rely on tone of voice more than just words or sound. They can be trained to react to a certain sound, at a certain volume. If you say "No, Oliver" in a very soft, pleasant voice, it will not have the same meaning as "No, Oliver!!" when you raise your voice.

You should never use the dog's name during a reprimand, just the command "No! " You never want the dog to associate his name with a negative experience or reprimand.

like, "Do you want this treat? You can do this, good dog." Your reassuring tone of voice will help calm the dog as he tries to follow the food hand in order to get the treat.

When the dog's elbows touch the floor, release the food and praise softly. Try to get the dog to maintain that down position for several seconds before you let him sit up again. The goal here is to get the dog to settle down and not feel threatened in the down position.

TEACHING STAY

It is easy to teach the dog to stay in either a sit or a down position. Again, we use food and praise during the teaching process as we help the dog to understand exactly what it is that we are expecting him to do.

To teach the sit/stay, start with the dog sitting on your left side as before and hold the lead in your left hand. Have a food treat in your right hand and place your food hand at the dog's nose. Say "Stay" and step out on your right foot to stand directly in front of the dog, toe to toe, as he licks and nibbles the treat. Be sure to keep his head facing upward to maintain the sit position. Count to five and then swing around to stand next to the dog again with him on your left. As soon as you get back to the original position, release the food

Once in the sit position, your Husky should not move from the position until you signal him to do so.

and praise lavishly.

To teach the down/stay, do the down as previously described. As soon as the dog lies down, say "Stay" and step out on your right foot just as you did in the sit/stay. Count to five and then return to stand beside the dog with him on your left side. Release the treat and praise as always.

Within a week or ten days, you can begin to add a bit of distance between you and your dog when you leave him. When you do, use your left hand open with the palm facing the dog as a stay signal, much the same as the hand signal a police officer uses to stop traffic at an intersection. Hold the food treat in your right hand as before, but this time the food is not touching the dog's nose. He will watch the food hand and quickly learn that he is going to get that treat as soon as you return to his side.

When you can stand 3 feet away from your dog for 30 seconds, you can then begin building time and distance in both stays. Eventually, the dog can be expected to remain in the stay position for prolonged periods of time until you return to him or call him to you. Always praise lavishly when he stays.

TEACHING COME

If you make teaching "Come" a fun experience, you should never have a "student" that does not love the game or that fails to come when called. The secret, it seems, is never to teach the word "come."

At times when an owner most wants his dog to come when called, the owner is likely upset or anxious and he allows these feelings to come through in the tone of his voice when he calls his dog. Hearing that desperation in his owner's voice, the dog fears the results of going to him and therefore either disobeys outright or runs in the opposite direction. The secret, therefore, is to teach the dog a game and, when you want him to come to you, simply play the game. It is practically a no-fail solution!

To begin, have several members of your family take a few food treats and each go into a different room in the house. Take turns calling the dog, and each person should celebrate the dog's finding him with a treat and lots of happy praise. When a person calls the dog, he is actually inviting the dog to find him and get a treat as a reward for "winning."

A few turns of the "Where are you?" game and the dog will figure out that everyone is playing the game and that each person has a big celebration awaiting his success at locating them. Once he learns to love the game, simply calling out "Where are you?" will bring him running from wherever he is when he hears that all-important question.

The come command is recognized as one of the most important things to teach a dog, so it is interesting to note that there are trainers who work with thousands of dogs and never teach the actual word "come." Yet these dogs will race to respond to a person who uses the dog's name followed by "Where are you?" In one instance, for example, a woman has a 12-year-old companion dog who went blind, but who never fails to locate her owner when asked, "Where are you?"

Children particularly love to play this game with their dogs. Children can hide in smaller places like a shower or bathtub, behind a bed or under a table.

The dog needs to work a little bit harder to find these hiding places, but, when he does, he loves to celebrate with a treat and a tussle with a favorite youngster.

TEACHING HEEL

Heeling means that the dog walks beside the owner without pulling. It takes time and patience on the owner's part to succeed at teaching the dog that he (the owner) will not proceed unless the dog is walking calmly beside him. Pulling out ahead on the lead is definitely not acceptable.

Begin with holding the lead in your left hand as the dog sits beside your left leg. Hold the loop end of the lead in your right hand but keep your left hand short on the lead so it keeps the dog in close next to you.

Say "Heel" and step forward on your left foot. Keep the dog close to you and take three steps. Stop and have the dog sit next to you in what we now call the heel position. Praise verbally, but do not touch the dog. Hesitate a

moment and begin again with "Heel," taking three steps and stopping, at which point the dog is told to sit again.

Your goal here is to have the dog walk those three steps without pulling on the lead. When he will walk calmly beside you for three steps without pulling, increase the number of steps you take to five. When he will walk politely beside you while you take five steps, you can increase the length of your walk to ten steps. Keep increasing the length of your stroll until the dog will walk quietly beside you without pulling as long as you want him to heel. When you stop heeling, indicate to the dog that the exercise is over by verbally praising as you pet him and say "OK, good dog." The "OK" is used as a release word, meaning that the exercise is finished and the dog is free to relax.

Your dog should comfortably keep pace beside you whether you walk or run. He should never be allowed to pull on the lead.

HEELING WELL

Teach your dog to heel in an enclosed area. Once you think the dog will obey reliably and you want to attempt advanced obedience exercises such as off-lead heeling, test him in a fenced-in area so he cannot run away.

never stops trying for that reward. No matter what, *always* give verbal praise.

OBEDIENCE CLASSES
As previously discussed, it is a good idea to enroll in an obedience class if one is available in your area. Many areas have dog clubs that offer basic obedience training as well as preparatory classes for obedience competition. There are also local dog trainers who offer similar classes.

At obedience trials, dogs can earn titles at various levels of competition. The beginning levels of competition include basic behaviors such as sit, down, heel, etc. The more advanced levels of competition include jumping, retrieving, scent discrimination and signal work. The advanced levels require a dog and owner to put a lot of time and effort into their training; the titles that can be earned at these levels of competition are very prestigious.

OTHER ACTIVITIES FOR LIFE
Whether a dog is trained in the structured environment of a class or alone with his owner at home, there are many activities that can bring fun and rewards to both owner and dog once they have mastered basic control.

Teaching the dog to help out around the home, in the yard or on the farm provides great satisfaction to both dog and

Photo by Kent & Donna Dannen.

Huskies were bred and trained for the purpose of pulling sleds for long distances in frigid temperatures. They still enjoy participating in sledding and other winter sports.

owner. In addition, the dog's help makes life a little easier for his owner and raises his stature as a valued companion to his family. It helps give the dog a purpose; it helps to keep his mind occupied and provides an outlet for his energy.

Backpacking is an exciting and healthful activity that the dog can be taught without assistance from more than his owner. The exercise of walking and climbing is good for man and dog alike, and the bond that they develop together is priceless.

If you are interested in participating in organized competition with your Siberian Husky, there are other activities other than obedience in which you and your dog can become involved. Agility is a popular and fun sport where dogs run through an obstacle course that includes various jumps, tunnels and other exer-

cises to test the dog's speed and coordination. The owners often run through the course beside their dogs to give commands and to guide them through the course. Although competitive, the focus is on fun—it's fun to do and fun to watch, as well as great exercise.

While every Husky owner will not be able to share in the excitement of a race like the Iditarod, owners easily can participate with their Huskies in fun winter sports. Building upon the dogs' natural abilities as sled dogs, owners can train their Huskies to do everything from sledding with the children to competing in sled-dog trials. For the ski aficionado, Huskies are great fun for skijoring as well. A vigorous play session in the snow will be heartily enjoyed by the Siberian Husky...he will feel right at home!

Talk about a working dog— dedicated, competitive and fun to watch. These Siberian Huskies are competing in a sled-dog race.

HEALTH CARE OF YOUR

SIBERIAN HUSKY

Dogs, being mammals like human beings, suffer from many of the same physical illnesses as people. They might even share many of the same psychological problems. Since people usually know more about human diseases than canine maladies, many of the terms used in this chapter will be the familiar terms, not necessarily those used by veterinarians. We'll still use the term *x-ray*, instead of the more acceptable term *radiograph*. We will also use the familiar term *symptoms* even though dogs don't have symptoms. Dogs have *clinical signs*. Symptoms, by the way, are verbal descriptions of the patient's feelings. Since dogs can't speak, we have to look for clinical signs...but we still use the term *symptoms* in this book.

As a general rule, medicine is *practiced*. That term is not arbitrary. Medicine is an art. It is a constantly changing art as we learn more and more about genetics, electronic aids (like CAT scans and MRIs) and research findings. There are dog maladies, like canine hip dysplasia, which are not universally treated in the same manner. Some veterinarians opt for surgery more often than others.

SELECTING A QUALIFIED VETERINARIAN

Your selection of a veterinarian should be based upon ability and personality as well as upon his convenience to your home. You want a vet who is close, as you might have emergencies or need multiple visits for treatments. You want a vet who has services that you might require such as a boarding kennel and grooming facilities; one who makes sophisticated pet supplies available and who has a good reputation for ability and responsiveness. There is nothing more frustrating than having to wait a day or more to get a response from a veterinarian.

All veterinarians are licensed and their diplomas and/or certificates should be displayed in their waiting rooms. There are, however, many veterinary specialties that usually require further studies and internships. There are specialists in heart problems (veterinary cardiologists), skin problems (veterinary dermatologists), teeth and gum problems (veterinary dentists), eye problems (veterinary ophthalmologists) and x-rays (veterinary radiologists), and surgeons who have specialties in bones, muscles or other organs. Most veterinarians do routine surgery such as neutering, stitching up wounds and docking tails for those breeds in which such is required for show purposes.

When the problem affecting your dog is serious, it is not unusual or impudent to get another medical opinion. You might also want to compare costs between several veterinarians. Sophisticated health care and veterinary services can be very costly. Do not be bashful about discussing these costs with your veterinarian or his staff. It is not infrequent that important decisions are based upon financial considerations.

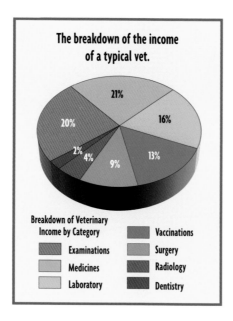

The breakdown of the income of a typical vet.

21%
16%
20%
2%
4%
9%
13%

Breakdown of Veterinary Income by Category

- Examinations
- Medicines
- Laboratory
- Vaccinations
- Surgery
- Radiology
- Dentistry

PREVENTATIVE MEDICINE

It is much easier, less costly and more effective to practice preventative medicine than to fight bouts of illness and disease.

Properly bred puppies come from parents that were selected based upon their genetic disease profiles. Their mother should have been vaccinated, free of all internal and external parasites and properly nourished. For these reasons, a visit to the veterinarian who cared for the dam (mother) is recommended. The dam can pass on disease resistance to her puppies. This resistance can last for eight to ten weeks. She can also pass on parasites and many infections. That is why you should learn as much about the dam's health as possible.

WEANING TO FIVE MONTHS OLD

Puppies should be weaned by the time they are about two months old. A puppy that remains for at least eight weeks with its mother and littermates usually adapts better to other dogs and people later in its life.

In every case, you should have your newly acquired puppy examined by a veterinarian immediately. Vaccination programs usually begin when the puppy is very young.

The puppy will have its teeth examined, its skeletal conformation checked and its general health checked prior to certification by the veterinarian. Many puppies have problems with cataracts and other eye problems, heart murmurs and undescended testicles. They may also have personality problems and your veterinarian might have training in temperament evaluation.

Vaccination Scheduling

Most vaccinations are given by injection and should only be done by a veterinarian. Both he and you should keep a record of the date of the injection, the identification of the vaccine and the amount given. The vaccination scheduling is based on a 15-day cycle. The first vaccinations should start when the puppy is 6–8 weeks old, then 15 days later when it is 10–12 weeks of age and later when it is 14–16 weeks of age. Vaccinations should *never* be given without a 15-day lapse between injections.

Most vaccinations immunize your puppy against viruses. The usual vaccines contain immunizing doses of several different viruses such as distemper, parvovirus, parainfluenza and hepatitis. There are other vaccines available when the puppy is at risk. You should rely upon professional advice. This is especially true for the booster-shot program. Most vaccination programs require a booster when the puppy is a year old, and once a year thereafter. In some cases,

PUPPY WORMING
Caring for the puppy starts before the puppy is born by keeping the dam healthy and well-nourished. Most puppies have worms, even if they are not evident, so a worming program is essential. The worms continually shed eggs except during their dormant stage, when they just rest in the tissues of the puppy. During this stage they are not evident during a routine examination.

circumstances may require more or less frequent immunizations.

Canine cough, more formally known as tracheobronchitis, is treated with a vaccine that is sprayed into the dog's nostrils. Canine cough is usually included in routine vaccination, but it is often not as effective as the vaccines for other major diseases. Your vet will explain and manage all details of the vaccination program.

Five Months to One Year of Age

By the time your puppy is five months old, he should have completed his vaccination program. During his physical examination, he should be evaluated for the common hip dysplasia plus other diseases of the joints. There are tests to assist in the prediction of these problems. Other tests can also be run, such as the parvovirus antibody titer, which can assess the effectiveness of the vaccination program.

Upon purchasing your Siberian Husky puppy, you must tell the breeder whether or not you intend to show and/or breed the dog. If you are seeking a Husky solely for pet companionship, you would be well advised to have the dog neutered. Neutering the puppy at six months of age is recommended; discuss this with your veterinarian. Neutering has proven to be extremely beneficial to both male and female puppies. Besides the obvious impossibility of pregnancy, it inhibits (but does not prevent) breast cancer in bitches and prostate cancer in male dogs.

Blood tests are performed for heartworm infestation and it is possible that your puppy will be placed on a preventative therapy, which will prevent heartworm infection as well as control other internal parasites.

DOGS OLDER THAN ONE YEAR

Continue to visit the veterinarian at least once a year. There is no such disease as old age, but bodily functions do change with age, and the eyes and ears are no longer as efficient. Neither are the internal workings of the liver, kidneys and intestines. Proper dietary changes, recommended by your veterinarian, can make life more pleasant for the aging Siberian Husky and you.

SKIN PROBLEMS IN SIBERIAN HUSKIES

Veterinarians are consulted by dog owners for skin problems more than any other group of diseases or maladies. Dogs' skin is almost as sensitive as human skin and both suffer almost the same ailments (though the occurrence of acne in dogs is rare!). For this reason, veterinary dermatology has developed into a specialty practiced by many veterinarians.

Since many skin problems have visual symptoms that are almost identical, it requires the skill of an experienced veterinary dermatologist to identify and cure many of the more severe skin disorders. Simply put, if your dog is suffering from a skin disorder, seek professional assistance as quickly as possible. As with all diseases, the earlier a problem is identified and treated, the more successful is the cure.

Pet shops sell many treatments for skin problems. Most of the treatments are simply directed at symptoms and not the underlying problem(s).

HEREDITARY SKIN DISORDERS

Veterinary dermatologists are currently researching a number of skin disorders that are believed to have a hereditary basis. These inherited diseases are transmitted by both parents, who appear (phenotypically)

HEALTH AND VACCINATION SCHEDULE

AGE IN WEEKS:	3RD	6TH	8TH	10TH	12TH	14TH	16TH	20-24TH
Worm Control	✔	✔	✔	✔	✔	✔	✔	✔
Neutering								✔
Heartworm		✔						✔
Parvovirus		✔		✔		✔		✔
Distemper			✔		✔		✔	
Hepatitis			✔		✔		✔	
Leptospirosis		✔		✔		✔		
Parainfluenza		✔		✔		✔		
Dental Examination			✔					✔
Complete Physical			✔					✔
Temperament Testing			✔					
Coronavirus					✔			
Canine Cough		✔						
Hip Dysplasia							✔	
Rabies								✔

Vaccinations are not instantly effective. It takes about two weeks for the dog's immune system to develop antibodies. Most vaccinations require annual booster shots. Your veterinarian should guide you in this regard.

normal but have a recessive gene for the disease, meaning that they carry, but are not affected by, the disease. These diseases pose serious problems to breeders because in some instances there is no method of identifying carriers. Often the secondary diseases associated with these skin conditions are even more debilitating than the disorder itself, including cancers and respiratory problems.

Among the hereditary skin disorders, for which the mode of inheritance is known, are acrodermatitis, cutaneous asthenia (Ehlers-Danlos syndrome), sebaceous adenitis, cyclic hematopoiesis, dermato-myositis, IgA deficiency, color dilution alopecia and nodular dermatofibrosis. Some of these disorders are limited to one or two breeds and others affect a large number of breeds. All inherited diseases must be diagnosed and treated by a veterinary specialist.

ZINC-RESPONSIVE DERMATOSIS
Siberian Huskies can have a genetic disorder that involves intestinal absorption of the mineral zinc. Zinc is an extremely important mineral for the body,

and its properties promote a healthy immune system. Certain skin disorders can be cleared by supplementing the Husky's diet with zinc and vitamin A. There are other breeds that share this type of disorder, including the Alaskan Malamute and Samoyed (likely the other Northern breeds as well). Diet also affects zinc absorption and owners are discouraged from using calcium supplements for Huskies.

PET ADVANTAGES

If you do not intend to show or breed your new puppy, your veterinarian will probably recommend that you spay your female or neuter your male. Some people believe neutering leads to weight gain, but if you feed and exercise your dog properly, this is easily avoided. Spaying or neutering can actually have many positive outcomes, such as:

• training becomes easier, as the dog focuses less on the urge to mate and more on you!
• females are protected from unplanned pregnancy, as well as ovarian and uterine cancers.
• males are guarded from testicular tumors and have a reduced risk of developing prostate cancer.

Talk to your vet regarding the right age to spay/neuter and other aspects of the procedure.

PARASITE BITES
Many of us are allergic to mosquito bites. The bites itch, erupt and may even become infected. Dogs have the same reaction to fleas, ticks and/or mites. When you feel the prick of the mosquito when it bites you, you have a chance to kill it with your hand. Unfortunately, when your dog is bitten by a flea, tick or mite, it can only scratch it away or bite it. By the time the dog has been bitten, the parasite has done some of its damage. It may also have laid eggs to cause further problems in the near future. The itching from parasite bites is probably due to the saliva injected into the site when the parasite sucks the dog's blood.

AUTO-IMMUNE SKIN CONDITIONS
Auto-immune skin conditions are commonly referred to as being allergic to yourself. Allergies, though, usually result in inflammatory reactions to an outside stimulus. Auto-immune diseases cause serious damage to the tissues which are involved.

The best known auto-immune disease is lupus. It affects people as well as dogs. The symptoms are very variable and may affect the kidneys, bones, blood chemistry and skin. It can be fatal to both dogs and humans, though it is not thought to be transmissible. It is usually successfully treated with cortisone, prednisone or similar corticosteroid, but extensive use of these drugs can have harmful side effects.

ACRAL LICK GRANULOMA
Siberian Huskies and other dogs of about the same size (like Labrador Retrievers) have a very poorly understood syndrome called acral lick. The manifestation of the problem is the dog's tireless attack at a specific area of the body, almost always the legs. The dog licks so intensively that he removes the hair and skin, leaving an ugly, large wound. There is no absolute cure, but corticosteroids are the most common treatment.

AIRBORNE ALLERGIES
Just as humans have hay fever, rose fever and other fevers from which they suffer during the pollinating season, many dogs suffer from the same allergies. So when the pollen count is high, your dog might suffer, but don't expect him to sneeze and have a runny nose like a human would. Dogs react to pollen allergies the same way they react to fleas—they scratch and bite themselves. Siberian Huskies are very susceptible to airborne pollen allergies.

Dogs, like humans, can be tested for allergens. Discuss the testing with a qualified veterinary dermatologist.

SIMULATED MEDICAL CONDITION FOR EDUCATIONAL PURPOSES ONLY.

Why a dog licks at a hot spot on its leg until the spot becomes infected is not known. Known as acral lick syndrome, this condition is treatable but not preventable.

FOOD ALLERGIES
Dogs are allergic to many foods that are best-sellers and highly recommended by breeders and veterinarians. Changing the brand of food that you buy may not eliminate the problem because the element of the food to which the dog is allergic may also be contained in the new brand.

Recognizing a food allergy is difficult. Humans vomit or have rashes when they eat a food to which they are allergic. Dogs neither vomit nor (usually) develop a rash. Instead they itch, scratch and bite, thus making the diagnosis extremely difficult. While pollen allergies and parasite bites are usually seasonal, food allergies are year-round problems.

TREATING FOOD PROBLEMS
Handling food allergies and food intolerance yourself is possible. Put your dog on a diet that it has

never had. Obviously if the dog has never eaten this new food, it can't have been allergic or intolerant of it. Start with a single ingredient that is *not* in the dog's diet at the present time. Ingredients like chopped beef or chicken are common in dog's diets, so try something more exotic like ostrich, rabbit, pheasant or some other quality source of protein. Keep the dog on this diet (with no additives) for a month. If the symptoms of food allergy or intolerance disappear, chances are that you have defined the cause.

Don't think that the single ingredient cured the problem. You still must find a suitable diet and ascertain which ingredient in the old diet was objectionable. This is most easily done by adding ingredients to the new diet one at a time until the problem is solved. Let the dog stay on the modified diet for a month before you add another ingredient.

An alternative method is to carefully study the ingredients in the diet to which your dog is allergic or intolerable. Identify the main ingredient in this diet and eliminate the main ingredient by buying a different food that does not have that ingredient. Keep experimenting until the symptoms disappear after one month on the new diet.

EXTERNAL PARASITES

FLEAS
Of all the problems to which dogs are prone, none is more well known and frustrating than fleas. Fleas, which usually refers to fleas, ticks and mites, are relatively simple to cure but difficult to prevent. The opposite is true for the parasites which are harbored inside the body. They are a bit more difficult to cure but they are easier to control.

It is possible to control flea infestation but you have to understand, the life cycle of a typical flea in order to control them. Basically, fleas are a summertime problem and their effective treatment (destruction) is environmental. The problem is that there is no single flea-control medicine (insecticide) that can be used in every flea-infested area. To understand flea control, you must apply suitable treatment to the weak link in the life cycle of the flea.

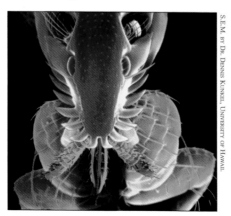

A scanning electron micrograph of a dog or cat flea, *Ctenocephalides*, magnified more than 100X. This has been colorized for effect.

S.E.M. BY DR. DENNIS KUNKEL, UNIVERSITY OF HAWAII.

Number-One Killer Disease in Dogs: CANCER

In every age, there is a word associated with a disease or plague that causes humans to shudder. In the 21st century, that word is "cancer." Just as cancer is the leading cause of death in humans, it claims nearly half the lives of dogs that die from a natural disease as well as half the dogs that die over the age of ten years.

Described as a genetic disease, cancer becomes a greater risk as the dog ages. Vets and dog owners have become increasingly aware of the threat of cancer to dogs. Statistics reveal that one dog in every five will develop cancer, the most common of which is skin cancer. Many cancers, including prostate, ovarian and breast cancer, can be avoided by spaying and neutering our dogs by the age of six months.

Early detection of cancer can save or extend a dog's life, so it is absolutely vital for owners to have their dogs examined by a qualified vet or oncologist immediately upon detection of any abnormality. Certain dietary guidelines have also proven to reduce the onset and spread of cancer. Foods based on fish rather than beef, due to the presence of Omega-3 fatty acids, are recommended. Other amino acids such as glutamine have significant benefits for canines, particularly those breeds that show a greater susceptibility to cancer.

Cancer management and treatments promise hope for future generations of canines. Since the disease is genetic, breeders should never breed a dog whose parents, grandparents and any related siblings have developed cancer. It is difficult to know whether to exclude an otherwise healthy dog from a breeding program, as the disease does not manifest itself until the dog's senior years.

RECOGNIZE CANCER WARNING SIGNS

Since early detection can possibly rescue your dog from becoming a cancer statistic, it is essential for owners to recognize the possible signs and seek the assistance of a qualified professional.

- Abnormal bumps or lumps that continue to grow
- Bleeding or discharge from any body cavity
- Persistent stiffness or lameness
- Recurrent sores or sores that do not heal
- Inappetence
- Breathing difficulties
- Weight loss
- Bad breath or odors
- General malaise and fatigue
- Eating and swallowing problems
- Difficulty urinating and defecating

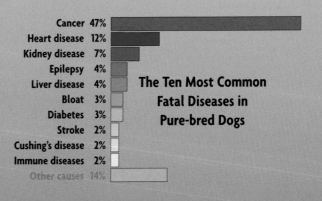

Disease	%
Cancer	47%
Heart disease	12%
Kidney disease	7%
Epilepsy	4%
Liver disease	4%
Bloat	3%
Diabetes	3%
Stroke	2%
Cushing's disease	2%
Immune diseases	2%
Other causes	14%

The Ten Most Common Fatal Diseases in Pure-bred Dogs

PHOTO BY DWIGHT R. KUHN.

An exceptional action photo showing a flea jumping from a dog's back.

THE LIFE CYCLE OF A FLEA

Fleas are found in four forms: eggs, larvae, pupae and adults. You really need a low-power microscope or magnifying glass to identify a living flea's eggs, pupae or larvae. Fleas spend their whole lives on your Siberian Husky unless they are forcibly removed by brushing, bathing, scratching or biting.

Several species infest both dogs and cats. The dog flea is scientifically known as *Ctenocephalides canis* while the cat flea is *Ctenocephalides felis*. Cat fleas are very common on dogs.

Fleas lay eggs while they are in residence on your dog. These eggs do not adhere to the hair of your dog and they simply fall off almost as soon as they dry (they may be a bit damp when initially laid). These eggs are the reservoir of future flea infestations. If your dog scratches himself and is able to dislodge a few fleas, they simply fall off and await a future chance to attack a dog...or even a person. Yes, fleas from dogs bite people. That's why it is so important to control fleas both on the dog and in the dog's entire environment. You must, therefore, treat the dog and the environment simultaneously.

DE-FLEAING THE HOME

Cleanliness is the simple rule. If you have a cat living with your dog, the matter is more complicated since most dog fleas are actually cat fleas. But since cats climb onto many areas that are never accessible to dogs (like window sills, table tops, etc.), you have to clean all of these areas, too. The hard floor surfaces (tiles, wood, stone and linoleum) must be mopped several times a day. Drops of food on the floor are actually food for flea larvae! All rugs and furniture must be vacuumed several times a day. Do not forget closets, under furniture and cushions. A study has reported that a vacuum cleaner with a beater bar can only remove 20% of the larvae and 50% of the

The Life Cycle of the Flea

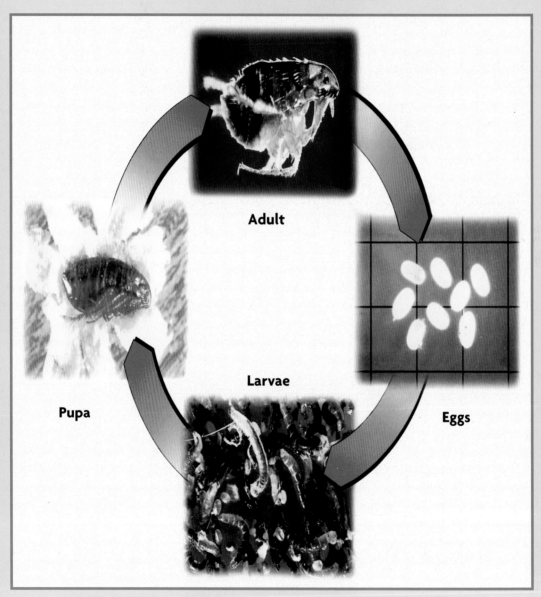

Adult

Eggs

Larvae

Pupa

The Life Cycle of the Flea was posterized by Fleabusters. Poster courtesy of Fleabusters®, Rx for Fleas.

A scanning electron micrograph (S.E.M.) of a dog flea, *Ctenocephalides canis.*

S.E.M. BY DR. DENNIS KUNKEL, UNIVERSITY OF HAWAII

eggs. The vacuum bags should be discarded into a sealed plastic bag or burned. The vacuum cleaner itself should be cleaned. The outdoor area to which your dog has access must also be treated with an insecticide.

This sounds like a lot of work! If you can afford it, you are better off hiring a professional to do it.

While there are many drugs available to kill fleas on the dog itself, it is best to have the de-fleaing of both the dog and the home supervised by your vet. Household sprays containing IGRs (Insect Growth Regulators) have been successful in eradicating eggs and larvae, while insecticides are available to kill adult fleas. There are currently no treatments available to attack the pupa stage so the adult insecticide is used to kill the newly hatched fleas before they find a host.

STERILIZING THE ENVIRONMENT
Besides cleaning your home with vacuum cleaners and mops, you have to treat the outdoor environment of your dog. This means trimming bushes, spreading insecticide and being careful not to poison areas in which other animals reside. This is best done by an outside service specializing in de-fleaing. Your vet should be able to recommend a local service.

TICKS AND MITES
Though not as common as fleas, ticks and mites are found all over the tropical and temperate world. They don't bite, like fleas; rather, they harpoon. They dig the sharp proboscis (nose) into the dog's skin and drink the blood. Their only food and drink is dog's blood. Dogs can get Lyme disease, Rocky Mountain spotted fever, paralysis and many other diseases from ticks and mites. They may live where fleas are found except they also like to hide in cracks or seams in walls. They are controlled the same way fleas are controlled.

The dog tick *Dermacentor variabilis* is the most common dog tick in many areas, especially those areas where the climate is hot and humid.

Most dog ticks have life expectancies of a week to six months, depending upon climatic conditions. They can neither jump nor fly, but they can crawl slowly and can travel up to 16 feet to reach a sleeping or unsuspecting dog.

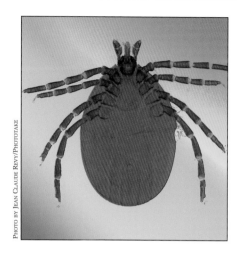

PHOTO BY JEAN CLAUDE REVY/PHOTOTAKE

MANGE

Mites cause a skin irritation called mange. Some are contagious, like *Cheyletiella*, ear mites, scabies and chiggers. The non-contagious mites are *Demodex*. The most serious of the mites is the type that infests dog's ears. Ear mites can be

controlled with treatments available from the vet. It is essential that your dog be treated for mange as quickly as possible because some forms of mange are transmissible to people.

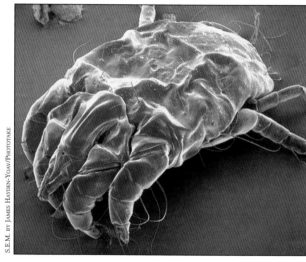

S.E.M. BY JAMES HAYDEN-YOAV/PHOTOTAKE

The dog tick of the genus *Ixode*.

INTERNAL PARASITES

Most animals—fishes, birds and mammals, including dogs and humans—have worms and other parasites which live inside their bodies. According to Dr. Herbert R. Axelrod, the fish pathologist, there are two kinds of parasites: dumb and smart. The smart parasites live in peaceful cooperation with their hosts (symbiosis), while the dumb parasites kill their hosts. Most of the worm infections are relatively easy to control. If they are not controlled, they weaken the host dog to the point that

Magnified view of the mange mite, *Psoroptes bovis*.

The dog tick, *Dermacentor variabilis*, is probably the most common tick found on dogs. Look at the strength in its eight legs! No wonder it's hard to detach them.

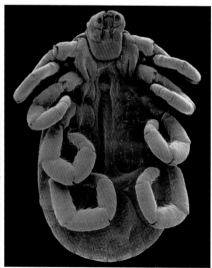

S.E.M. BY DR. DENNIS KUNKEL, UNIVERSITY OF HAWAII

other medical problems occur, but they are not dumb parasites.

ROUNDWORMS

Male and female hookworms, *Ancylostoma caninum.*

The roundworms that infect dogs are scientifically known as *Toxocara canis*. They live in the dog's intestines. The worms shed eggs continually. It has been estimated that a dog produces about 6 ounces of feces every day. Each ounce of feces averages 250,000–300,000 eggs of roundworms. There are no known areas in which dogs roam that do not contain roundworm eggs. The greatest danger of roundworms is that they infect people, too! It is wise to have your dog tested regularly for roundworms.

The roundworm can infect both dogs and humans.

PHOTO BY CAROLINA BIOLOGICAL SUPPLY/PHOTOTAKE

Pigs also have roundworm infections that can be passed to human and dogs. The typical roundworm parasite is called *Ascaris lumbricoides*.

HOOKWORMS

The worm *Ancylostoma caninum* is commonly called the dog hookworm and is dangerous to

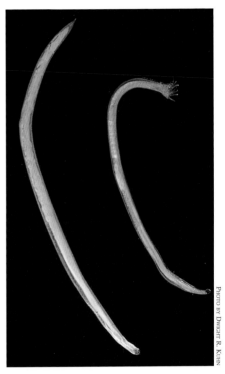

PHOTO BY DWIGHT R. KUHN

humans and cats. It also has teeth by which it attaches itself to the intestines of the dog. Because it changes the site of its attachment about six times a day, the dog loses blood from each detachment, possibly causing iron-deficiency anemia. They are rarely found on pet or show dogs, though they can be a problem for dogs that have access to grasslands, usually sheepdogs and racing Greyhounds.

TAPEWORMS

There are many species of tapeworms. They are carried by fleas! The dog eats the flea and thus starts the tapeworm cycle. Humans can also be infected with tapeworms, so don't eat fleas! Fleas are so small that your dog could pass them onto your hands, your plate or your food and thus make it possible for you to ingest a flea that is carrying tapeworm eggs.

While tapeworm infection is not life-threatening in dogs (smart parasite!), it can be the cause of a very serious liver disease for humans. About 50 percent of the humans infected with *Echinococcus multilocularis*, causing alveolar hydatis, perish.

HEARTWORMS

Heartworms are thin, extended worms up to 12 inches long, which live in a dog's heart and major blood vessels around the heart. Siberian Huskies may have up to 200 of these worms. The symptoms may be loss of energy, loss of appetite, coughing, the development of a pot belly and anemia.

Heartworms are transmitted by mosquitoes. The mosquito drinks the blood of an infected dog and takes in larvae with the blood. The larvae, called microfilaria, develop within the body of the mosquito and are

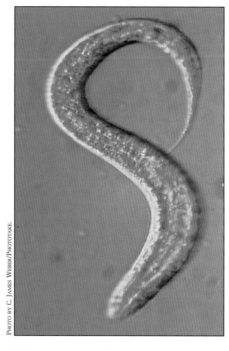

PHOTO BY C. JAMES WEBER/PHOTOTAKE.

The infective stage of the hookworm larva.

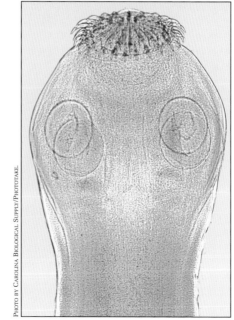

PHOTO BY CAROLINA BIOLOGICAL SUPPLY/PHOTOTAKE.

The head and rostellum (the round prominence on the scolex) of a tapeworm, which infects both dogs and humans.

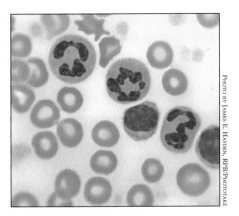

Magnified heartworm larvae, *Dirofilaria immitis*.

PHOTO BY JAMES E. HAYDEN, RPB/PHOTOTAKE

passed on to the next dog bitten after the larvae mature. It takes two to three weeks for the larvae to develop to the infective stage within the body of the mosquito. Dogs should be treated at about six weeks of age, then every six months.

Blood testing for heartworms is not necessarily indicative of how seriously your dog is infected. Discuss preventative measures with your vet.

This surgically opened dog's heart is infected with canine heartworm, *Dirofilaria immitis*.

PHOTO BY C. JAMES WEBB/PHOTOTAKE

DO YOU KNOW ABOUT HIP DYSPLASIA?

Hip dysplasia is a fairly common condition found in Siberian Huskies, as well as other breeds. When a dog has hip dysplasia, his hind leg has an incorrectly formed hip joint. By constant use of the hip joint, it becomes more and more loose, wears abnormally and may become arthritic.

Hip dysplasia can only be confirmed with an x-ray, but certain symptoms may indicate a problem. Your Siberian Husky may have a hip dysplasia problem if he walks in a peculiar manner, hops instead of smoothly running, uses his hinds legs in unison (to keep the pressure off the weak joint), has trouble getting up from a prone position and always sits with both legs together on one side of his body.

As the dog matures, he may adapt well to life with a bad hip, but in a few years the arthritis develops and many Siberian Huskies with hip dysplasia become cripples.

Hip dysplasia is considered an inherited disease and can usually be diagnosed when the dog is three to nine months old. Some experts claim that a special diet might help your puppy outgrow the bad hip, but the usual treatments are surgical. These include the removal of the pectineus muscle, the removal of the round part of the femur, reconstructing the pelvis and replacing the hip with an artificial one. All of these surgical interventions are expensive, but they are usually very successful. Follow the advice of your veterinarian.

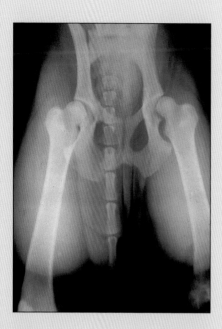

Hip Dysplasia

Compare the two hip joints and you'll understand dysplasia better. Hip dysplasia is a badly worn hip joint caused by improper fit of the bone into the socket. It is easily the most common hip problem in Siberian Huskies.

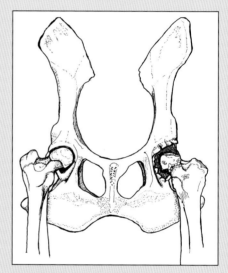

The healthy hip joint on the right and the unhealthy hip joint on the left.

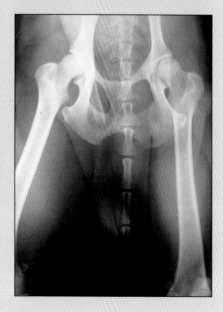

Hip dysplasia can only be positively diagnosed by x-ray. Siberian Huskies manifest the problem when they are between four and nine months of age, the so-called fast-growth period.

MEDICAL PROBLEMS MOST FREQUENTLY SEEN IN SIBERIAN HUSKIES

Condition	Age Affected	Cause	Area Affected
Acral Lick Granuloma	Any age, males	Unknown	Legs and paws
Cataracts	Any age	Hereditary	Eyes
Crystalline Corneal Opacities	Puppy/young dogs	Hereditary	Eyes
Elbow Dysplasia	4 to 7 mos.	Congenital	Elbow joint
Gastric Dilatation (Bloat)	Older dogs	Swallowing air	Stomach
Glaucoma	1 year and up	Hereditary	Eyes
Hip Dysplasia	By 2 years	Congenital	Hip joint
Progressive Retinal Atrophy	Any age	Hereditary	Retinal tissue/eyes
Zinc-Responsive Dermatosis	Adults	Congenital	Skin/Intestines

First Aid
at a Glance

Burns
Place the affected area under cool water; use ice if only a small area is burnt.

Bee stings/Insect bites
Apply ice to relieve swelling; antihistamine dosed properly.

Animal bites
Clean any bleeding area; apply pressure until bleeding subsides; go to the vet.

Spider bites
Use cold compress and a pressurized pack to inhibit venom's spreading.

Antifreeze poisoning
Immediately induce vomiting by using hydrogen peroxide.

Fish hooks
Removal best handled by vet; hook must be cut in order to remove.

Snake bites
Pack ice around bite; contact vet quickly; identify snake for proper antivenin.

Car accident
Move dog from roadway with blanket; seek veterinary aid.

Shock
Calm the dog, keep him warm; seek immediate veterinary help.

Nosebleed
Apply cold compress to the nose; apply pressure to any visible abrasion.

Bleeding
Apply pressure above the area; treat wound by applying a cotton pack.

Heat stroke
Submerge dog in cold bath; cool down with fresh air and water; go to the vet.

Frostbite/Hypothermia
Warm the dog with a warm bath, electric blankets or hot water bottles.

Abrasions
Clean the wound and wash out thoroughly with fresh water; apply antiseptic.

 Remember: an injured dog may attempt to bite a helping hand from fear and confusion. Always muzzle the dog before trying to offer assistance.

CDS: COGNITIVE DYSFUNCTION SYNDROME
"Old-Dog Syndrome"

There are many ways for you to evaluate old-dog syndrome. Veterinarians have defined CDS (cognitive dysfunction syndrome) as the gradual deterioration of cognitive abilities. These are indicated by changes in the dog's behavior. When a dog changes his routine response, and maladies have been eliminated as the cause of these behavioral changes, then CDS is the usual diagnosis.

More than half the dogs over eight years old suffer from some form of CDS. The older the dog, the more chance he has of suffering from CDS. In humans, doctors often dismiss the CDS behavioral changes as part of "winding down."

There are four major signs of CDS: frequent potty accidents inside the home, sleeping much more or much less than normal, acting confused and failing to respond to social stimuli.

SYMPTOMS OF CDS

FREQUENT POTTY ACCIDENTS
- *Urinates in the house.*
- *Defecates in the house.*
- *Doesn't signal that he wants to go out.*

SLEEP PATTERNS
- *Moves much more slowly.*
- *Sleeps more than normal during the day.*
- *Sleeps less during the night.*

CONFUSION
- *Goes outside and just stands there.*
- *Appears confused with a faraway look in his eyes.*
- *Hides more often.*
- *Doesn't recognize friends.*
- *Doesn't come when called.*
- *Walks around listlessly and without a destination.*

FAILURE TO RESPOND TO SOCIAL STIMULI
- *Comes to people less frequently, whether called or not.*
- *Doesn't tolerate petting for more than a short time.*
- *Doesn't come to the door when you return home.*

SIBERIAN HUSKY

The term *old* is a qualitative term. For dogs, as well as their masters, old is relative. Certainly we can all distinguish between a puppy Siberian Husky and an adult Siberian Husky—there are the obvious physical traits such as size and appearance, and personality traits like their antics and the expressions on their faces. Puppies and young dogs like to play with children. Children's natural exuberance is a good match for the seemingly endless energy of young dogs. They like to run, jump, chase and retrieve. When dogs grow up and cease their interaction with children, they are often thought of as being too old to play with the kids.

Siberian Huskies are active dogs who remain vigorous and energetic until they are eight or nine years of age. They slowly "wind down" and eventually become easygoing and calm companions.

If people live to be 100 years old, dogs live to be 20 years old. While this is a good rule of thumb, it is very inaccurate. When trying to compare dog years to human years, you cannot make a generalization about all dogs. You can make the generalization that, say, 13 years is a good lifespan for a Siberian Husky, but you cannot compare it to that of a Chihuahua, as many small breeds typically live longer than large breeds. Dogs are generally considered mature within three years. They can reproduce even earlier. So the first three years of a dog's life are more like seven times that of comparable humans. That means a three-year-old dog is like a 21-year-old person. As the curve of comparison shows, there is no hard and fast rule for comparing dog and human ages. The comparison is made even more difficult, for not all humans age at the same rate...and human females live longer than human males.

It is very difficult to ascertain a Husky's age by looking at his face. His body language, such as slow, belabored movement, is more indicative.

SENIOR SIGNS

Your Husky will slowly develop signs to tell you that his body and mind are slowing down. Your senior Husky may start to show one or more of the following symptoms:

- The hair on the face and paws starts to turn gray. The color breakdown usually starts around the eyes and mouth.
- Sleep patterns are deeper and longer, and the old dog is harder to awaken.
- Food intake diminishes.
- Responses to calls, whistles and other signals are ignored more and more.
- Eye contact does not evoke tail wagging (assuming it once did).

WHAT TO LOOK FOR IN SENIORS

Most veterinarians and behaviorists use the seven-year mark as the time to consider a dog a "senior." The term "senior" does not imply that the dog is geriatric and has begun to fail in mind and body. Aging is essentially a slowing process. Humans readily admit that they feel a difference in their activity level from age 20 to 30, and then from 30 to 40, etc. By treating the seven-year-old dog as a senior, owners are able to implement certain therapeutic and preventive medical strategies with the help of their veterinarians. A senior-care program should include at least two veterinary visits per year, screening sessions to determine the dog's health

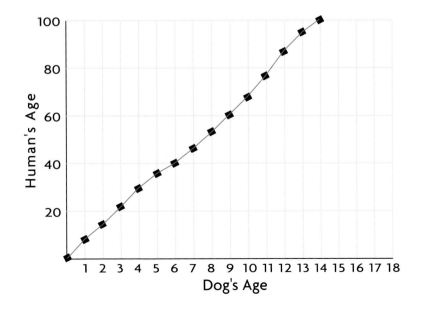

Senior dogs require special attention from owner and vet alike. Your vet can prescribe a preventative care program for your senior Husky.

status, as well as nutritional counseling. Veterinarians determine the senior dog's health status through a blood smear for a complete blood count, serum chemistry profile with electrolytes, urinalysis, blood pressure check, electrocardiogram, ocular tonometry (pressure on the eyeball) and dental prophylaxis.

Such an extensive program for senior dogs is well advised before owners start to see the obvious physical signs of aging, such as slower and inhibited movement, graying, increased sleep/nap periods and disinterest in play and other activity. This

GETTING OLD

The bottom line is simply that your dog is getting old when you think he is getting old because he slows down in his level of general activity, including walking, running, eating, jumping and retrieving. On the other hand, the frequency of certain activities increases, such as more sleeping, more barking and more repetition of habits like going to the door without being called when you put your coat on to leave the house.

preventative program promises a longer, healthier life for the aging dog. Among the physical problems common in aging dogs are the loss of sight and hearing, arthritis, kidney and liver failure, diabetes mellitus, heart disease and Cushing's disease (a hormonal disease).

In addition to the physical manifestations discussed, there are some behavioral changes and problems related to aging dogs. Dogs suffering from hearing or vision loss, dental discomfort or arthritis can become aggressive.

NOTICING THE SYMPTOMS

The symptoms listed below are symptoms that gradually appear and become more noticeable. They are not life-threatening; however, the symptoms below are to be taken very seriously and warrant a discussion with your veterinarian:

• Your dog cries and whimpers when he moves, and he stops running completely.

• Convulsions start or become more serious and frequent. The usual convulsion (spasm) is when the dog stiffens and starts to tremble, being unable or unwilling to move. The seizure usually lasts for 5 to 30 minutes.

• Your dog drinks more water and urinates more frequently. Wetting and bowel accidents take place indoors without warning.

• Vomiting becomes more frequent.

Likewise the near-deaf and/or blind dog may be startled more easily and react in an unexpectedly aggressive manner. Seniors suffering from senility can become more impatient and irritable. Housesoiling accidents are associated with loss of mobility, kidney problems, loss of sphincter control, as well as plaque accumulation, physiological brain changes and reactions to medications. Older dogs, just like young puppies, suffer from separation anxiety, which can lead to excessive barking, whining, housesoiling and destructive behavior. Seniors may become fearful of everyday sounds, such as vacuum cleaners, heaters, thunder and passing traffic. Some dogs have difficulty sleeping, due to discomfort, the need for frequent potty visits and the like.

Owners should avoid spoiling the older dog with too many fatty treats. Obesity is a common problem in older dogs and subtracts years from their lives. Keep the senior dog as trim as possible since excessive weight puts additional stress on the body's vital organs. Some breeders recommend supplementing the diet with foods high in fiber and lower in calories. Adding fresh vegetables and marrow broth to the senior's diet makes a tasty, low-calorie, low-fat supplement. Vets also offer

Cemeteries for pets exist. Consult your veterinarian to help you locate one.

specialty diets for senior dogs that are worth exploring.

Your dog, as he nears his twilight years, needs his owner's patience and good care more than ever. Never punish an older dog for an accident or abnormal behavior. For all the years of love, protection and companion-ship that your dog has provided, he deserves special attention and courtesies. The older dog may need to relieve himself at 3 a.m. because he can no longer hold it for eight hours. Older dogs may not be able to remain crated for more than two or three hours. It may be time to give up a sofa or chair to your old friend. Although he may not seem as enthusiastic about your attention and petting, he does appreciate the considerations you offer as he gets older.

Your Husky does not understand why his world is slowing down. Owners must make the transition into the golden years as pleasant and rewarding as possible.

WHAT TO DO WHEN THE TIME COMES

You are never fully prepared to make a rational decision about putting your dog to sleep. It is very obvious that you love your Siberian Husky or you would not be reading this book. Putting a loved dog to sleep is extremely difficult. It is a decision that must be made with your veterinarian.

EUTHANASIA

Euthanasia must be performed by a licensed veterinarian. There also may be societies for the prevention of cruelty to animals in your area. They often offer this service upon a vet's recommendation.

Whether your Siberian Husky is a perfect show dog, like this Best of Breed winner, or just a good typical specimen of the breed, dog shows offer a very rewarding and exciting sport for human and canine alike.

SHOWING YOUR
SIBERIAN HUSKY

When you purchase your Siberian Husky, you will make it clear to the breeder whether you want one just as a loveable companion and pet, or if you hope to be buying a Siberian Husky with show prospects. No reputable breeder will sell you a young puppy and tell you that it is *definitely* of show quality, for so much can go wrong during the early months of a puppy's development. If you plan to show, what you will hopefully have acquired is a puppy with "show potential."

To the novice, exhibiting a Siberian Husky in the show ring may look easy, but it takes a lot of hard work and devotion to do top winning at a show such as the prestigious Westminster Kennel Club dog show, not to mention a little luck too!

The first concept that the canine novice learns when watching a dog show is that each dog first competes against members of its own breed. Once the judge has selected the best member of each breed (Best of Breed), that chosen dog will compete with other dogs in its group. Finally, the dogs chosen first in each group will compete for Best in Show.

The second concept that you must understand is that the dogs are not actually compared against one another. The judge compares each dog against its breed standard, the written description of the ideal specimen that is approved by the American Kennel Club (AKC). While some early breed standards were indeed based on specific dogs that were famous or popular, many dedicated enthusiasts say that a perfect specimen, as described in the standard, has never walked into

Anyone can give dog showing a try. Familiarize yourself with show procedure and etiquette, and consider having a breeder evaluate your dog's potential in the ring...then go for it!

a show ring, has never been bred and, to the woe of dog breeders around the globe, does not exist. Breeders attempt to get as close to this ideal as possible with every litter, but theoretically the "perfect" dog is so elusive that it is impossible. (And if the "perfect" dog were born, breeders and judges would never agree that it was indeed "perfect.")

If you are interested in exploring the world of dog showing, your best bet is to join your local breed club or the national parent club, which is the Siberian Husky Club of

The Best of Breed Siberian Husky has won over all other Huskies entered in the show in all classs and both sexes.

America. These clubs often host both regional and national specialties, shows only for Siberian Huskies, which can include conformation as well as obedience and agility trials. Even if you have no intention of competing with your Husky, a specialty is like a festival for lovers of the breed who congregate to share their favorite topic: Huskies! Clubs also send out

newsletters and some organize training days and seminars in order that people may learn more about their chosen breed. To locate the breed club closest to you, contact the AKC, which furnishes the rules and regulations for all of these events plus general dog registration and other basic requirements of dog ownership.

The AKC offers three kinds of conformation shows: an all-breed show (for all AKC-recognized breeds), a specialty show (for one breed only, usually sponsored by the parent club) and a Group show (for all breeds in the Group).

For a dog to become an AKC champion of record, the dog must accumulate 15 points at the shows from at least three different judges, including two "majors." A "major" is defined as a three-, four- or five-point win, and the number of points per win is determined on the number of dogs entered in the show on the day. Depending on the breed, the number of points that are awarded varies. In a breed as popular as the Siberian Husky, more dogs are needed to rack up the points. At any dog show, only one dog and one bitch of each breed can win points.

Dog showing does not offer "co-ed" classes. Dogs and bitches never compete against each other in the classes. Non-champion dogs are called "class dogs" because they compete in one of five classes. Dogs are entered in a particular class

Two winning Huskies pose with their handlers and the judge at an outdoor show.

depending on its age and previous show wins. To begin, there is the Puppy Class (for 6- to 9-month-olds and for 9- to 12-month-olds); this class is followed by the Novice Class (for dogs that have not won any first prizes except in the Puppy Class or three first prizes in the Novice Class and have not accumulated any points toward their champion title); the Bred-by-Exhibitor Class (for dogs handled by their breeders or handled by one of the breeder's immediate family); American-bred Class; and the Open Class (for any dog that is not a champion).

The judge at the show begins judging the Puppy Class, first dogs

MEET THE AKC

The American Kennel Club is the main governing body of the dog sport in the United States. Founded in 1884, the AKC consists of 500 or more independent dog clubs plus 4,500 affiliate clubs, all of which follow the AKC rules and regulations. Additionally, the AKC maintains a registry for pure-bred dogs in the US and works to preserve the integrity of the sport and its continuation in the country. Over 1,000,000 dogs are registered each year, representing about 150 recognized breeds. There are over 15,000 competitive events held annually for which over 2,000,000 dogs enter to participate. Dogs compete to earn over 40 different titles, from champion to Master Agility Champion.

INFORMATION ON CLUBS

You can get information about dog shows from the national kennel clubs:

American Kennel Club
5580 Centerview Dr., Raleigh, NC 27606-3390
www.akc.org

United Kennel Club
100 E. Kilgore Road, Kalamazoo, MI 49002
www.ukcdogs.com

Canadian Kennel Club
89 Skyway Ave., Suite 100, Etobicoke
Ontario, M9W 6R4 Canada
www.ckc.ca

The Kennel Club
1-5 Clarges St., Piccadilly,
London W1Y 8AB, UK
www.the-kennel-club.org.uk

and then bitches, and proceeds through the classes. The judge places his winners first through fourth in each class. In the Winners Class, the first-place winners of each class compete with one another to determine Winners Dog and Winners Bitch. The judge also places a Reserve Winners Dog and Reserve Winners Bitch, which could be awarded the points in the case of a disqualification. The Winners Dog and Winners Bitch, the two that are awarded the points for the breed, then compete with any champions of record entered in the show. The judge reviews the Winners Dog, Winners Bitch and all the other

Working Group competition: the Group One dog is an Alaskan Malamute (front) and the Group Two dog is a Siberian Husky (behind). It's interesting to note the difference in size and build between the two dogs.

Eight magnificent Huskies racing. There's nothing subjective about this kind of competition. It does not rely upon a judge's opinion, but upon who finishes the trail first.

champions to select his Best of Breed. The Best of Winners is selected between the Winners Dog and Winners Bitch. Were one of these two to be selected Best of Breed, it would automatically be named Best of Winners as well. Finally the judge selects his Best of Opposite Sex to the Best of Breed winner.

At a Group show or all-breed show, the Best of Breed winners from each breed then compete against one another for Group One through Group Four. The judge compares each Best of Breed to its breed standard and the dog that most closely lives up to the ideal for its breed is selected as Group One. Finally, all seven group winners (from the Working Group, Toy Group, Hound Group, etc.) compete for Best in Show.

To find out about dog shows in your area, you can subscribe to the American Kennel Club's monthly magazine, The *American Kennel Gazette* and the accompanying *Events Calendar*. You can also look in your local newspaper for advertisements for dog shows in your area or go on the Internet to the AKC's website, www.akc.org.

If your Siberian Husky is six months of age or older and registered with the AKC, you can

FIVE CLASSES AT SHOWS

At most AKC all-breed shows, there are five regular classes offered: Puppy, Novice, Bred by Exhibitor, American-bred and Open. The Puppy Class is usually divided as 6- to 9-months of age and 9- to 12-months of age. When deciding which class to enter your dog, male or female, you must carefully check the show schedule to make sure that you have selected the right class. Depending on the age of the dog, its previous first-place wins and the sex of the dog, you must make the best choice. It is possible to enter a one-year-old dog who has not won sufficient first places in any of the non-Puppy Classes, though the competition is more intense.

enter him in a dog show where the breed is offered classes. Provided that your Siberian Husky does not have a disqualifying fault, he can compete. Only unaltered dogs can be entered in a dog show, so if you have spayed or neutered your Siberian Husky, you cannot compete in conformation shows. The reason for this is simple. Dog shows are the main forum to prove which representatives in a breed are worthy of being bred. Only dogs that have achieved championships—the AKC "seal of approval" for quality in pure-bred dogs—should be bred. Altered dogs, however, can

participate in other AKC events such as obedience trials and the Canine Good Citizen® program.

Before you actually step into the ring, you would be well advised to sit back and observe the judge's ring procedure. If it is your first time in the ring, do not be over-anxious and run to the front of the line. It is much better to stand back and study how the exhibitor in front of you is performing. The judge asks each handler to "stack" the dog, hopefully showing the dog off to his best advantage. The judge will observe the dog from a distance and from different angles, and approach the dog to

The race begins with the dogs struggling to get the sled moving. These tests truly evaluate a Husky's working ability.

PHOTO BY KENT & DONNA DANNEN

Once the sled gets going, the Huskies run faster and faster and build themselves up to a fever pitch.

check his teeth, overall structure, alertness and muscle tone, as well as consider how well the dog "conforms" to the standard. Most importantly, the judge will have the exhibitor move the dog around the ring in some pattern that he should specify (another advantage to not going first, but always listen since some judges change their directions—and the judge is always right!). Finally, the judge will give the dog one last look before moving on to the next exhibitor.

If you are not in the top four in your class at your first show, do not be discouraged. Be patient and consistent and you may eventually find yourself in a winning line-up. Remember that the winners were once in your shoes and have devoted many hours and much money to earn the placement. If you find that your dog is losing every time and never getting a nod, it may be time to consider a different dog sport or to just enjoy your Siberian Husky as a pet. Parent clubs offer non-conformation events, which may be of interest to the owner of a well-trained Siberian Husky.

OBEDIENCE TRIALS

Obedience trials in the US trace back to the early 1930s when organized obedience training was developed to demonstrate how well dog and owner could work together. The pioneer of obedience trials is Mrs. Helen Whitehouse Walker, a Standard Poodle fancier, who designed a series of exercises after the Associated Sheep, Police Army Dog Society of Great Britain. Since the days of Mrs. Walker, obedience trials have grown by leaps and bounds, and today there are over 2,000 trials held in the US every year, with more than 100,000 dogs competing. Any registered AKC dog can enter an obedience trial, regardless of conformational disqualifications or neutering.

Obedience trials are divided into three levels of progressive difficulty. At the first level, the Novice, dogs compete for the title Companion Dog (CD); at the intermediate level, the Open, dogs compete for the title Companion Dog Excellent (CDX); and at the advanced level, dogs compete for the title Utility Dog (UD).

AGILITY TRIALS

Having had its origins in the UK back in 1977, AKC agility had its official beginning in the US in August 1994, when the first licensed agility trials were held. The AKC allows all registered breeds (including Miscellaneous Class breeds) to participate, providing the dog is 12 months

Patty Sansom races her Siberian Huskies in Granby, Colorado. Her Huskies can be traced back to the original sled dogs that Leonard Seppala brought to Alaska from Russia.

PHOTO BY KENT & DONNA DANNEN

A team of six Huskies race in this magnificent scene.

of age or older. The handler directs his dog over an obstacle course that includes jumps as well as tires, the dog walk, weave poles, pipe tunnels, collapsed tunnels, etc. While working their way through the course, the dog must keep one eye and ear on the handler and the rest of his body on the course. The handler gives verbal and hand signals to guide the dog through the course.

The first organization to promote agility trials in the US was the United States Dog Agility Association, Inc. (USDAA), which was established in 1986 and spawned numerous member clubs around the country. Both the USDAA and the AKC offers titles to winning dogs. Three titles are available through the USDAA: Agility Dog (AD), Advanced Agility Dog (AAD) and Master Agility Dog (MAD). The AKC offers Novice Agility (NA), Open Agility (OA), Agility Excellent (AX) and Master Agility Excellent (MX). Beyond these four AKC titles, dogs can win additional ones in "jumper" classes, which lead to the ultimate title(s): MACH, Master Agility Champion. Dogs can continue to add number designations to the MACH titles, indicating how many times the dog has met the MACH requirements.

This highly trained Husky is quite a performer. Here, he demonstrates some of his skills at an outdoor festival.

As a Siberian Husky owner, you have selected your dog so that you and your loved ones can have a companion, a protector, a friend and a four-legged family member. You invest time, money and effort to care for and train the family's new charge. Of course, this chosen canine behaves perfectly! Well, *perfectly* like a dog.

THINK LIKE A DOG

Dogs do not think like humans, nor do humans think like dogs, though we try. Unfortunately, a dog is incapable of figuring out how humans think, so the responsibility falls on the owner to adopt a proper canine mindset. Dogs cannot rationalize and dogs exist in the present moment. Many dog owners make the mistake in training of thinking that they can reprimand a dog for something he did a while ago. Basically, you cannot even reprimand a dog for something he did 20 seconds ago! Either catch him in the act or forget it! It is a waste of your time and your dog's time—in his mind, you are reprimanding him for whatever he is doing at that moment.

The following behavioral problems represent some which owners most commonly encounter. Every dog is unique and every situation is unique. No author could purport for you to solve your Siberian Husky's problem simply by reading a script. Here we outline some basic "dogspeak" so that owners' chances of solving behavioral problems are increased. Discuss bad habits with your veterinarian and he/she can recommend a behavioral specialist to consult in appropriate cases. Since behavioral abnormalities are the leading reason that owners abandon their pets, we hope that

Puppies learn the principles of the pack through interaction and play.

you will make a valiant effort to solve your Siberian Husky's problem. Patience and understanding are virtues that should dwell in every pet-loving household.

> ### DOGGIE DEMOCRACY
> Your dog inherited the pack-leader mentality. He only knows about pecking order. He instinctively wants to be "top dog," but you have to convince him that you are boss. There is no such thing as living in a democracy with your dog. You are the one who makes the rules.

AGGRESSION

Aggression can be a very big problem in dogs. Aggression, when not controlled, becomes dangerous. An aggressive dog, no matter the size, may lunge at, bite or even attack a person or another dog. Aggressive behavior is not to be tolerated. It is more than just inappropriate behavior; it is not safe with any dog. It is painful for a family to watch their dog become unpredictable in his behavior to the point where they are afraid of the dog. And while not all aggressive behavior is dangerous, it can be frightening: growling, baring teeth, etc. It is important to get to the root of the problem to ascertain why the dog is acting in this manner. Aggression is a display of dominance, and the dog should

Aggression within a team is completely unacceptable. These dogs must be unquestionably reliable.

not have the dominant role in his pack, which is, in this case, your family.

It is important not to challenge an aggressive dog as this could provoke an attack. Observe your Siberian Husky's body language. This is a primitive, natural breed. Huskies absolutely know how to communicate their minds through their bodies. Does he make direct eye contact and stare? Does he try to make himself as large as possible: ears pricked, chest out, tail proudly furled? Height and size signify authority in a dog pack—being taller or "above" another dog literally means that he is "above" in the social status. These body signals tell you that

PHOTO BY KENT & DONNA DANNEN

cause of your dog's aggression and do something about it. An aggressive dog cannot be trusted, and a dog that cannot be trusted is not safe to have as a family pet. If the pet Siberian Husky becomes untrustworthy, he cannot be kept in the home with the family. The family must get rid of the dog. In the very worst case, the dog must be euthanized.

Barking is not necessarily a sign of aggression, it is simply a dog's way of communicating verbally.

Just look at this puppy! A born leader.

your Siberian Husky thinks he is in charge, a problem that needs to be dealt with. An aggressive dog is unpredictable in that you never know when he is going to strike and what he is going to do. You cannot understand why a dog that is playful and loving one minute is growling and snapping the next.

The best solution is to consult a behavioral specialist, one who has experience with the Siberian Husky if possible. Together, perhaps you can pinpoint the

SET AN EXAMPLE
Never shout, jump or run about if you want your dog to stay calm. Huskies can be quite excitable and need to learn when it's time to play and when they should be calm. You set the example for your dog's behavior in most circumstances. Learn from your dog's reactions and act accordingly.

AGGRESSION TOWARD OTHER DOGS
A dog's aggressive behavior toward another dog stems from not enough exposure to other dogs at an early age. If other dogs make your Siberian Husky nervous and agitated, he will lash out as a protective mechanism. A dog who has not received sufficient exposure to other canines tends to believe that he is the only dog on the planet. The animal becomes so dominant that he does not even show signs that he is fearful or threatened. Without growling or any other physical signal as a warning, he will lunge at and bite

Today a pup on a playground... tomorrow an agility champion! As puppies play and grow, they develop coordination skills.

the other dog. A way to correct this is to let your Siberian Husky approach another dog when walking on lead. Watch very closely and at the very first sign of aggression, correct your Siberian Husky and pull him away. Scold him for any sign of discomfort and then praise him when he ignores or tolerates the other dog. Keep this up until either he stops the aggressive behavior, learns to ignore the other dog or even accepts other dogs. Praise him lavishly for his correct behavior.

DOMINANT AGGRESSION

A social hierarchy is firmly established in a wild dog pack. The dog wants to dominate those under him and please those above him. Dogs know that there must be a leader. If you are not the obvious choice for emperor, the dog will assume the throne! These conflicting innate desires are what a dog owner is up against when he sets about training a dog. In training a dog

to obey commands, the owner is reinforcing that he is the top dog in the "pack" and that the dog should, and should want to, serve his superior. Thus, the owner is suppressing the dog's urge to dominate and making him obedient.

An important part of training is taking every opportunity to reinforce that you are the leader. The simple action of making your Siberian Husky sit to wait for his food instead of allowing him to run up to get it when he wants it says that you control when he eats; he is dependent on you for food.

Although it may be difficult, do not give in to your dog's wishes every time he whines at you or looks at you with pleading eyes. It is a constant effort to show the dog that his place in the pack is at the bottom. This is not meant to sound cruel or inhumane. You love your Siberian Husky and you should treat him with care and affection. You

NO BUTTS ABOUT IT!

Dogs get to know each other by sniffing each other's backsides. It seems that each dog has a telltale odor, probably created by the anal glands. It also distinguishes sex and signals when a female will be receptive to a male's attention. Some dogs snap at another dog's intrusion of their private parts.

(hopefully) did not get a dog just so you could boss around another creature. Dog training is not about being cruel or feeling important, it is about molding the dog's behavior into what is acceptable and teaching him to live by your rules. In theory, it is quite simple: catch him in appropriate behavior and reward him for it. Add a dog into the equation and it becomes a bit more trying, but as a rule of thumb, positive reinforcement is what works best.

With a dominant dog, punishment and negative reinforcement can have the opposite effect of what you are after. It can make a dog fearful and/or act out aggressively if he feels he is being challenged. Remember, a dominant dog perceives himself at the top of the social heap and will fight to defend his perceived status. The best way to prevent that is to never give him reason to think that he is in control in the first place. If you are having trouble training your Siberian Husky and it seems as if he is constantly challenging your authority, seek the help of an obedience trainer or behavioral specialist. A professional will work with both you and your dog to teach you effective techniques to use at home. Beware of trainers who rely on excessively harsh methods; scolding is necessary now and then, but the focus in your training should always be on

NO EYE CONTACT

DANGER! If you and your on-lead dog are approached by a larger, running dog that is not restrained, walk away from the dog as quickly as possible. Do not allow your dog to make eye contact with the other dog. You should not make eye contact either. In dog terms, eye contact indicates a challenge.

positive reinforcement.

If you can isolate what brings out the fear reaction, you can help the dog get over it. Supervise your Siberian Husky's interactions with people and other dogs, and praise the dog when it goes well. If he starts to act aggressively in a situation, correct him and remove

Huskies require exercise or they may find other, less productive, ways to expend their energy.

PHOTO BY KENT & DONNA DANNEN

SOUND BITES

When a dog bites, there is always a good reason for his doing so. Many dogs are trained to protect a person, an area or an object. When that person, area or object is violated, the dog will attack. A dog attacks with his mouth. He has no other means of attack.

Fighting dogs (and there are many breeds which fight) are taught to fight, but they also have a natural instinct to fight. This instinct is normally reserved for other dogs, though unfortunate accidents can occur; for example, when a baby crawls toward a fighting dog and the dog mistakes the crawling child as a potential attacker.

If a dog is a biter for seemingly no reason, if he bites the hand that feeds him or if he snaps at members of your family, see your veterinarian or behaviorist immediately to learn how to modify the dog's behavior.

behavior by rewarding him when he acts appropriately. By being gentle and by supervising his interactions, you are showing him that there is no need to be afraid or defensive.

SEXUAL BEHAVIOR

Dogs exhibit certain sexual behaviors that may have influenced your choice of male or female when you first purchased your Siberian Husky. Spaying/neutering will eliminate these behaviors, but if you are purchasing a dog that you wish to breed, you should be aware of what you will have to deal with throughout the dog's life.

Female dogs usually have two estruses per year, each season lasting about three weeks. These are the only times in which a female dog will mate and she usually will not allow this until the second week of the cycle. If a bitch is not bred during the heat cycle, it is not uncommon for her to experience a false pregnancy, in which her mammary glands swell and she exhibits maternal tendencies toward toys or other objects.

Owners must further recognize that mounting is not merely a sexual expression but also one of dominance seen in males and females alike. Be consistent and persistent and you will find that you can "move mounters."

him from the situation. Do not let people approach the dog and start petting him without your express permission. That way, you can have the dog sit to accept petting and praise him when he behaves properly. You are focusing on praise and on modifying his

PHOTO BY KENT & DONNA DANNEN

"Dog boxes" are the usual way of holding sled dogs while they wait their turn to race. For dogs that are trained for sledding, this is as ordinary as a dog crate is for a pet or show dog.

CHEWING

The national canine pastime is chewing! Every dog loves to sink his "canines" into a tasty bone! Dogs need to chew, to massage their gums, to make their new teeth feel better and to exercise their jaws. This is a natural behavior deeply imbedded in all things canine. Our role as owners is not to stop chewing, but to redirect it to positive, chew-worthy objects. Be an informed owner and purchase safe chew toys for your Siberian Husky, like strong nylon bones made for large dogs. Be sure that the devices are safe and durable, since your dog's safety is at risk. Again, the owner is responsible for ensuring a dog-proof environment. The best answer is preven-tion: that is, put your shoes, handbags and other tasty objects in their proper places (out of the reach of the growing canine

FEAR IN A GROWN DOG

Fear in a grown dog is often the result of improper or incomplete socializa-tion as a pup, or it can be the result of a traumatic experience he suffered when young. Keep in mind that the term "traumatic" is relative—something that you would not think twice about can leave a lasting negative impression on a puppy. If the dog experiences a similar experience later in life, he may try to fight back to protect himself. Again, this behavior is very unpredictable, especially if you do not know what is triggering his fear.

Dogs need to chew, and Huskies are no exception. Get a safe chew toy from your local pet shop.

mouth). Direct puppies to their toys whenever you see them tasting the furniture legs or your pant leg. Make a loud noise to attract the pup's attention and immediately escort him to his chew toy and engage him with the toy for at least four minutes, praising and encouraging him all the while.

Some trainers recommend deterrents, such as hot pepper or another bitter spice or a product designed for this purpose, to discourage the dog from chewing on unwanted objects. This is sometimes reliable, though not as often as the manufacturers of such products claim. Test out the product with your own dog before investing in a case of it.

JUMPING UP

Jumping up is a dog's friendly way of saying hello! Some dog owners do not mind when their dog jumps up, which is fine for them. The problem arises when guests come to the house and the dog greets them in the same manner—whether they like it or not! However friendly the greeting may be, chances are your visitors will not appreciate nearly being knocked over by 45-50 lbs. of Husky. The

THE MIGHTY MALE

Males, whether castrated or not, will mount almost anything: a pillow, your leg or, much to your dismay, even your neighbor's leg. As with other types of inappropriate behavior, the dog must be corrected while in the act, which for once is not difficult. Often he will not let go! While a puppy is experimenting with his very first urges, his owners feel he needs to "sow his oats" and allow the pup to mount. As the pup grows into a full-size dog, with full-size urges, it becomes a nuisance and an embarrassment. Males always appear as if they are trying to "save the race," more determined and stronger than imaginable. While altering the dog at an appropriate age will limit the dog's desire, it usually does not remove it entirely.

dog will not be able to distinguish upon whom he can jump and whom he cannot. Therefore, it is probably best to discourage this behavior entirely.

Pick a command such as "Off" (avoid using "Down" since you will use that for the dog to lie down) and tell him "Off" when he jumps up. Place him on the ground on all fours and have him sit, praising him the whole time. Always lavish him with praise when he is in the sit position. That way you are still giving him a warm affectionate greeting.

DIGGING

Digging, which is seen as a destructive behavior to humans, is actually quite a natural behavior in dogs, especially in Siberian Huskies. Even though your dog is not one of the "earth dogs" (also known as terriers), his desire to dig can be irrepressible and most frustrating to his owners. When digging occurs in your yard, it is actually a normal behavior redirected into something the dog can do in his everyday life. For example, in the wild, a dog would be actively seeking food, making his own shelter, etc. He would be using his paws in a purposeful manner; he would be using them for his survival. Since you provide him with food and shelter, he has no need to use his paws for these purposes, and

NO JUMPING

Stop a dog from jumping up before he jumps. If he is getting ready to jump onto you, simply walk away. If he jumps up on you before you can turn away, lift your knee so that it bumps him in the chest. Do not be forceful. Your dog soon will realize that jumping up is not a productive way of getting attention.

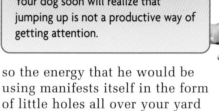

so the energy that he would be using manifests itself in the form of little holes all over your yard and flower beds.

Perhaps your dog is digging as a reaction to boredom—it is somewhat similar to your eating a whole bag of chips in front of the TV—because they are there and there is not anything better to do! Basically, the answer is to provide the dog with adequate play and exercise so that his mind and paws are occupied,

Huskies jump up as an expression of enthusiasm. This dog jumps up to say, "Welcome home! I missed you!"

Every dog is special and unique. Most owners of Siberian Huskies do not experience problems with their dogs' behavior, but it is always to be prepared for any possible problems.

and so that he feels as if he is doing something useful.

Of course, digging is easiest to control if it is stopped as soon as possible, but it is often hard to catch a dog in the act, especially if he is alone in the yard during the day. If your dog is a compulsive digger and is not easily distracted by other activi-

WARNING SIGNS

If your dog barks menacingly or growls at strangers, or if he growls at anyone who comes near his food while he is eating, playing with a toy or taking a rest in his favorite spot, he needs proper professional training because sooner or later this behavior can result in someone being bitten.

ties, you can designate an area on your property where it is okay for him to dig. If you catch him digging in an off-limits area of the yard, immediately bring him to the approved area and praise him for digging there. Keep a close eye on him so that you can catch him; that is the only way he is going to understand what is permitted and what is not. If you bring him to a hole he dug an hour ago and tell him "No," he will understand that you are not fond of holes, or dirt or flowers. If you catch him while he is stifle-deep in your tulips, that is when he will get your message.

BARKING

Barking is a dog's way of "talking," and the Siberian Husky has so much to say that you may even hear him howl! It can be somewhat frustrating because it is not always easy to tell what a dog means by his bark—is he

If you live with multiple dogs, they all should be disciplined and should behave well with each other.

excited, happy, frightened, angry? Whatever it is that the dog is trying to say, he should not be punished for barking. It is only when the barking becomes excessive, and when the excessive barking becomes a bad habit, that the behavior needs to be modified. If an intruder came into your home in the middle of the night and the dog barked a warning, wouldn't you be pleased? You would probably deem your dog a hero, a wonderful guardian and protector of your home. On the other hand, if a friend drops by unexpectedly and rings the doorbell and is greeted with a sudden sharp bark, you would probably be annoyed at the dog. But isn't it just the same behavior? The dog does not know any better... unless he sees who is at the door and it is someone with whom he

SMILE!

Dogs and humans may be the only animals that smile. A dog will imitate the smile on his owner's face when he greets a friend. The dog only smiles at his human friends; he never smiles at another dog or cat. Usually, a dog rolls up his lips and shows his teeth in a clenched mouth while rolling over onto his back, begging for a soft scratch.

is familiar, he will bark as a means of vocalizing that his (and your) territory is being threatened. While your friend is not posing a threat, it is all the same to the dog. Barking is his means of letting you know that there is an intrusion, whether friend or foe, on your property. This type of barking is instinctive and should not be discouraged.

Excessive habitual barking, however, is a problem that should be corrected early on. As your Siberian Husky grows up, you will be able to tell when his barking is purposeful and when it is for no reason. You will become able to distinguish your dog's different barks and with what they are associated. For example, the bark when someone comes to the door will be different from the bark when he is excited to see you. It is similar to a person's tone of voice, except that the dog has to rely totally on tone of voice because he does not have the benefit of using words. An incessant barker will be evident at an early age.

There are some things that encourage a dog to bark. For example, if your dog barks non-stop for a few minutes and you give him a treat to quiet him, he believes that you are rewarding him for barking. He will associate barking with getting a treat and will keep doing it until he is rewarded.

FOOD STEALING

Is your dog devising ways of stealing food from your counter tops? If so, you must answer the following questions: Is your Siberian Husky hungry, or is he "constantly famished" like every other chow hound? Why is there food on the counter top? Face it, some dogs are more food-motivated than others; some dogs are totally obsessed by a slab of meat and can only think of their next meal. Food stealing is terrific fun and always yields a great reward—*food*, glorious food!

The owner's goal, therefore, is to make the "reward" less rewarding, even startling! Plant a shaker can (an empty tin can with coins inside) on the counter so that it catches your pooch off-guard. There are other devices available that will surprise the dog

TRAINING TIP

To encourage proper barking, you can teach your dog the command "Quiet." When someone comes to the door and the dog barks a few times, praise him. Talk to him soothingly and, when he stops barking, tell him "Quiet" and continue to praise him. In this sense, you are letting him bark his warning, which is an instinctive behavior, and then rewarding him for being quiet after a few barks. You may initially reward him with a treat after he has been quiet for a few minutes.

This Siberian Husky is tired of waiting...he's howling to show that he's ready for the race to begin.

PHOTO BY KENT & DONNA DANNEN

Whether it's food or objects around the house, your Husky may steal things that arouse his interest. Of course, this is a habit that needs to be corrected early on.

when he is looking for a mid-afternoon snack. Such remote-control devices, though not the first choice of some trainers, allow the correction to come from the object instead of the owner. These devices are also useful to keep the snacking hound from napping on furniture that is forbidden.

BEGGING

Just like food stealing, begging is a favorite pastime of hungry puppies! With that same reward—*food!* Dogs quickly learn that their owners keep the "good food" for themselves and that we humans do not dine on kibble alone. Begging is a conditioned response related to a specific stimulus, time and place. The sounds of the

kitchen, cans and bottles opening, crinkling bags, the smell of food in preparation, etc., will excite the dog and soon the paws are in the air!

Here is the solution to stopping this behavior: Never give in to a beggar! You are rewarding the dog for sitting pretty, jumping up, whining and rubbing his nose into you by giving him that glorious reward—food. By ignoring the dog, you will (eventually) force the behavior into extinction. Note that the behavior likely gets worse before it disappears, so be sure there are not any softies in the family who will give in to little "Oliver" every time he whimpers, "More, please."

SEPARATION ANXIETY

Your Siberian Husky may howl, whine or otherwise vocalize his displeasure at your leaving the house and his being left alone. This is a normal case of separa-tion anxiety, but there are things that can be done to eliminate this problem. Your dog needs to learn that he will be fine on his own for a while and that he will not wither away if he is not attended to every minute of the day. In fact, constant attention can lead to separation anxiety in the first place. If you are endlessly coddling and pampering your dog, he will come to expect this from you all of the time and it will be more traumatic for him when you are not there. Obviously, you enjoy spending time with your dog and he thrives on your love and attention. However, it should not become a dependent relation-

goodbye and do not lavish him with hugs and kisses when you return. This is giving in to the attention that he craves and it will only make him miss it more when you are away. Another thing you

Well-behaved Huskies are cozy in their "dog boxes" while they await the beginning of the sled race.

ship where he is heartbroken without you.

One thing you can do to minimize separation anxiety is to make your entrances and exits as low-key as possible. Do not give your dog a long drawn-out

can try is to give your dog a treat when you leave; this will not only keep him occupied and keep his mind off the fact that you just left, but it will also help him associate your leaving with a pleasant experience.

You may have to accustom your dog to being left alone in intervals, much like when you introduced your pup to his crate. When your dog starts whimpering as you approach the door, your first instinct will be to run to him and comfort him, but do not do it! His anxiety stems from being placed in an unfamiliar situation; by familiarizing him with being alone, he will learn that he is okay. That is not to say you should purposely leave your dog home alone, but the dog needs to know that while he can depend on you for his care, you do not have to be by his side 24 hours a day.

When the dog is alone in the house, he should be confined to his crate or a designated dog-proof area of the house. This should be the area in which he sleeps, so he should already feel comfortable there and this should make him feel more at ease when he is alone. This is just one of the many examples in which a crate is an invaluable tool for you and your dog, and another reinforcement of why your dog should view his crate as a "happy" place, a place of his own.

COPROPHAGIA
Feces eating is, to most humans, one of the most disgusting behaviors that their dog could engage in, yet to the dog it is perfectly normal. It is hard for us to understand why a dog would want to eat its own feces; he could be seeking certain nutrients that are missing from his diet, he could be just plain hungry, or he could be attracted by the pleasing (to a dog) scent.

While coprophagia most often refers to the dog's eating his own feces, a dog may likely eat that of another animal as well if he comes across it. Vets have found that diets with a low digestibility, containing relatively low levels of fiber and high levels of starch, increase coprophagia. Therefore, high-fiber diets may decrease the likelihood of dogs' eating feces. Both the consistency of the stool (how firm it feels in the dog's mouth) and the presence of undigested nutrients increase the likelihood. Dogs often find the stool of cats and horses more palatable than that of other dogs. Once the dog develops diarrhea from feces eating, he will likely quit this distasteful habit, since dogs tend to prefer eating harder feces.

To discourage this behavior, first make sure that the food you are feeding your dog is nutritionally complete and that he is getting enough food. If changes in his diet do not solve the problem, and no medical cause can be found, you will have to modify the behavior through environmental control. There are some tricks you can try, such as adding an unpleasant-tasting substance to the feces to make them unpalatable or adding something to the dog's food which will make it unpleasant tasting after it passes through the dog. The best way to prevent your dog from eating his stool is to make it unavailable—clean up after he eliminates and remove any stool from the yard. If it is not there, he cannot eat it.

Never reprimand the dog for stool eating, as this rarely impresses the dog. Vets recommend distracting the dog while he is in the act of stool eating. Another option is to muzzle the dog when he is in the yard to relieve himself; this usually is effective within 30 to 60 days. Coprophagia most frequently is seen in pups 6 to 12 months of age, and usually disappears around the dog's first birthday.

A musher and his team of Huskies race over a frozen lake as they pass by Grays and Torrys Peaks, Colorado. The peaks are 14,250 feet in elevation.

PHOTO BY KENT & DONNA DANNEN.

My Siberian Husky

PUT YOUR PUPPY'S FIRST PICTURE HERE

Dog's Name _____

Date _____ Photographer _____